Waterst
guide to
Children's
Books

W

Contents

Where The Wild Things Are P.25

Introduction 3

How to use this guide 4

Pre-School Reading 5

- Baby Books
- Early Learning
- First Experiences
- Nursery Rhymes
- Pop-Ups and Novelties
- Picture Books

Young Readers 5-8 year olds 29

- Picture Books
- Reading Series
- Story Books

Fairy Tales and Mythology 43

Reading 8-12 year olds 49

- Authors A-Z
- Anthologies

Poetry 87

- Anthologies
- Poets

Reference 97

Young Adults 103

- Authors A-Z
- Teenage Health
- Series Fiction
- Further Reading

Subject Index 116

Prize Winners 120

Author & title Index 121

**Waterstone's
Branch Addresses** 126

Introduction

'We can give our children no greater gift than to open their eyes and minds to the infinite richness, the beauty and the excitement of our language and literature.' PD JAMES

What little coverage of children's books there has been in the Press in recent years has tended to be negative. Critics bemoan the decline in reading standards and the proliferation of formulaic series on the bookshelves. Prophets of doom foretell the imminent death of the children's book in a brave new world of multi-media.

This is not our experience at Waterstone's. What we have found is that the world of children's books is more vibrant than ever. 7,000 new titles are published each year, classics continue to sell, new authors still emerge and children continue to read.

Computers and video games cannot replace the experience of losing yourself in a book. The wonder of discovering new worlds, the thrill of undertaking magical journeys, the joys of revelling in the rhymes of Dr Seuss or Michael Rosen or of entering the dream worlds of CS Lewis or Roald Dahl are all still best experienced in the pages of a book.

From Aesop's animals to Toad of Toad Hall to Peter Pan, classic characters from children's literature are embedded in our culture. Contemporary children's books are thriving and we can confidently predict that Matilda, Flat Stanley and the Very Hungry Caterpillar will be regarded as equally influential classics by future generations.

What is wonderful about children's books today is the sheer variety on offer. For the Waterstone's Guide to Children's Books we have chosen and reviewed what we consider to be the very best of classic and contemporary books for children.

The focus of the guide is the world of fiction, although we have put together a small 'home library' of reference books. We hope there will be something for every child. There is also a subject index for special needs and interests. Ask our booksellers for advice; the books they have chosen for this guide are just a select few from the wide range we stock in our departments.

Above all, we hope this guide is an exciting introduction to the world of children's literature and that you will use it to foster an enthusiasm and love for books in your child.

We're Going on a Bear Hunt P.24

How to use this guide

Each book review is presented in the following format:

TITLE
Author/illustrator
Publisher, cover (hardback or paperback) and price
ISBN - to order the book

Review written by booksellers

4-6  ☆

The symbols above represent: An approximate guide to the
reading age, the book is available on tape, and the book has
won an award.
The Guide is divided into 7 main sections, roughly
chronological by age.
The subject index will help you with special needs and interests.
There is also an author and title index.
All books in the Guide can be obtained through
Waterstone's, subject to availability.
The reading age is not always given. Sometimes it is self
explanatory (all titles in 'Young Adults' are for 12-15 year olds),
and sometimes the age range is unrestricted.

First Fairy Tales P.46

Pre School

Pre-School

A love of books can be nurtured from a very early age. Babies love to play with soft and tactile books, and to point to shapes and objects in a story.

As they become toddlers they will recognise shared circumstances and eventually familiar emotions and feelings. At this stage, reading as a shared experience is crucial. A story at bedtime is a wonderful introduction to the world of children's books as well as an initiation into the possibilities of imaginary worlds.

We have chosen a range of books for pre-school children which covers everything from first ABC books to classic picture books (like Where's Spot? and Where the Wild Things Are), to hilarious pop-ups and traditional nursery rhymes.

Picture book illustration in Britain has always been renowned and there is now a more exciting choice than ever. The range of illustrative styles in use extends from Dick Bruna's two-dimensions and flat colours to award - winning water-colours and oils from Helen Oxenbury and Gary Blythe.

We have chosen books that make wonderful bedtime stories, that stimulate discussion and laughter and that have a visual style that works for children and not just for adults.

The Tiger who came to Tea P.20
Previous page: Oliver's Vegetables P.18

Baby Books

SNAPSHOT BOARD BOOKS
Dorling Kindersley

Chewable and durable, these perfect first-word books use simple text and clear photographs to encourage the identification of everyday objects.

WIBBLY PIG
Mick Inkpen
Hodder Children's Books £2.99

Reader and child will delight in the adventures of Wibbly Pig. Mick Inkpen's inimitable style appeals to every child. For more great Mick Inkpen books see page 19.

ELMER BATH BOOKS
David McKee
Random House Children's Books £3.99

Elmer is a patchwork elephant who shows very young children that it's alright to be different from everyone else.

Also available as picture books

WINNIE THE POOH CLOTH BOOKS
AA Milne
Reed Children's Books £2.99

Two bright and cheerful cloth books teaching children their first words through the characters of Pooh and friends. Safe, non-toxic and totally hand washable, these are perfect for a first dribble into reading!

NURSERY BOARD BOOKS
Jan Pienkowski
Reed Children's Books £1.99 - £2.50

Boldly illustrated simple first word books for children. This series of colourful board books will teach your child a whole range of first words from ABC to happy and sad.

FIRST FOCUS BABY BOOKS
Ladybird £1.99 - £2.99

Ladybird's First Focus range is the product of extensive research into a child's early years. Ladybird use strong, contrasting colours and bold black and white images to help develop your child's ability to focus on a variety of shapes, thus enhancing their visual awareness.

Available in a variety of formats from concertina cloth books, ideal for tying across your baby's cot, to squeaky bath books and shake and play books, all are guaranteed to stimulate a child's first interest in reading.

Early Learning

MY FIRST BOOK OF TIME
Dorling Kindersley hbk £8.99
ISBN 0863187846

Packed with information and easily accessible games and activities, with clear photographs and text. Comes with a special fold-out clock.

Wibbly Pig

MY FIRST WORD BOOK
Angela Wilkes
Dorling Kindersley £7.99
ISBN 0863186300

A first picture dictionary containing over 1,000 words commonly used by young children. The clear photographs illustrating each word encourage easy recognition whilst the thematic design stimulates discussion. This book will help with simple vocabulary building as well as counting and early reading.

LETTERLAND ABC

Collins hbk £8.99
ISBN 017410166X

Letterland is a very special place where children can see letters brought vividly to life through colourful characters. Extremely stimulating text and illustrations make this an invaluable introduction to the alphabet.

Lucy and Tom's ABC

THE FIRST THOUSAND WORDS

Heather Amery & Stephen Cartwright
Usborne hbk £5.99
ISBN 0746023022

Usborne's new, revised edition of 'First Thousand Words' provides the young reader with a fun and clear way to learn new words. A straightforward but also stimulating way to learn the language.

LUCY AND TOM'S ABC

Shirley Hughes
Puffin pbk £3.99
ISBN 0140505210

Shirley Hughes's delightful third book in this series takes children of any age through the alphabet. Each letter is depicted by everyday, homely situations. Every page is rich with traditional illustrations which reveal the warmth and happiness of childhood.

Did you Know?

Shirley Hughes began writing when her children were small because she felt there weren't many books available that were suitable for young children. Her first book, 'Lucy and Tom's Day' was published in 1960 and was followed by award-winners like 'Doggers' and 'Helpers'.

First Experiences

USBORNE FIRST EXPERIENCES

Anne Civardi & Stephen Cartwright
Usborne pbk £2.50 - £2.99

An excellent series of simple stories which introduce young children to new situations which they find difficult to understand. Amongst 'First Experiences' covered are flying, visiting the dentist and moving house.

GOING TO PLAYSCHOOL

Sarah Garland
Puffin pbk £3.99
ISBN 0140553630

Sarah Garland takes the fear out of that first day at playschool with bright and comforting illustrations and simple text.

ON YOUR POTTY!

Virginia Miller
Walker Books pbk £3.99
ISBN 0744531411

Playful and independent Bartholomew says "Nah" to everything - that is until he says "Aah" and earns himself a great big bear hug.

I WANT MY POTTY

Tony Ross
Collins pbk £4.50
ISBN 0006626874

Tony Ross encapsulates the madcap adventures of any family toilet-training its child. This is a perfect introduction to the wonders of potties for any child under 5 years old.

Did you Know?

Virginia Miller's most popular books are about small bear Ba and his father George. As well as 'On Your Potty', you can read about them in 'Get into Bed!' and 'Eat your Dinner!'. The Daily Telegraph called them 'the cuddliest of the season's publications'.

HOW DO I PUT IT ON?
Shigeo Watanabe
Red Fox pbk £3.50
ISBN 0099999404

A simple but valuable story of a young bear learning how to dress himself. The text is easy to follow, enhanced by repetitive phrases and light hearted illustrations. Good for reading together.

Nursery Rhymes

PLAYTIME TREASURY
Selected by Pie Corbett,
Kingfisher hbk £8.95
ISBN 0862724341

A collection of active and clapping rhymes, games, ring dances and songs. The pictures illustrate the words and actions of each rhyme and there are brief notes to explain the rules of each game.

RHYMES & LULLABIES
Vanessa Clarke
Kingfisher hbk £8.99
ISBN 0862722225

An illustrated collection of rhymes and nursery songs, suitable for babies and toddlers.

MOTHER GOOSE
Compiled & illustrated by
Michael Foreman
Walker Books hbk £14.99
ISBN 0744507758

Over 200 favourite nursery rhymes beautifully illustrated in Michael Foreman's own distinctive style.

NURSERY RHYMES
Jonathan Langley
Collins pbk £3.99
ISBN 0006641326

One of the best paperback anthologies of familiar rhymes, including Little Bo-Peep and Pease Pudding Hot.

THIS LITTLE PUFFIN
Elizabeth Matterson
Puffin pbk £4.99
ISBN 0140340483

A comprehensive source book of rhymes and songs for young children. Music is often included, as well as suggestions on how to play the games.

READ ALOUD RHYMES FOR THE VERY YOUNG
ed Jack Prelutsky
Walker hbk £12.99
ISBN 0744507707

A selection of over 200 short poems taken from the everyday world of young children that will capture their attention and fuel their imaginations.

OXFORD NURSERY RHYMES FOR THE VERY YOUNG
Sarah Williams & Ian Beck
Oxford UP pbk £2.99 each

Four individual collections of familiar songs and rhymes to suit even the youngest child. Titles include 'Round and Round the Garden' and 'Oranges and Lemons'.

Pop-Ups & Novelty Books

THE JOLLY POSTMAN (or Other People's Letters)
Janet & Allan Ahlberg
Methuen hbk £8.99
ISBN 0434925152

A children's classic. Follow the Jolly Postman on his rounds and actually pull out and read the letters he delivers!
4–6

Mother Goose

ALPHABUGS
David Carter
Orchard hbk £10.99
ISBN 1852137355

Alphabugs is an educational
pop-up book which manages
to make you laugh while you
learn.
4-6

MAISY GOES TO BED
ISBN 0744504295

MAISY GOES TO
PLAYSCHOOL
Lucy Cousins
Walker Books hbk £6.99
ISBN 074525063

These books form part of a
series of delightful interactive
stories about Maisy the
mouse. Children pull tabs
and lift flaps as they help
Maisy get ready for bed or
have fun at playschool. The
pictures are bold and bright
and the flaps are sturdy
enough to withstand the
onslaught of little hands.
up to 4

THE MOST AMAZING HIDE
& SEEK ALPHABET BOOK
Robert Crowther
Viking hbk £12.99
ISBN 0670489964

A journey through the
alphabet which is particularly
suitable for children who
enjoy searching for details
in pictures.
5-8

LADYBIRD MOVES HOME
Richard Fowler
Transworld hbk £5.99
ISBN 0385403828

Adopt the role of ladybird
as you guide her along her
path of words. An ingeniously
simple idea which aids
dexterity and encourages
inventive story telling.
up to 4 ☆

SAM'S SANDWICH
David Pelham
Cape hbk £5.99
ISBN 0224030116

Naughty Sam makes her
sister a sandwich full of
nasty surprises. Good fun!
Sam has more adventures in
'Sam's Surprise' and 'The
Sensational Samburger'.
4-6

Jan Pienkowski

*Jan Pienkowski has written
and illustrated dozens of
picture and pop-up books
to delight all ages. Many of
them, such as the Meg and
Mog series (with Helen
Nicoll) and the Robot pop-
up, are now acknowledged
as contemporary classics.*

HAUNTED HOUSE
Jan Pienkowski
Reed hbk £10.99
ISBN 043495635X

Haunted House has
monsters, ghouls and things
that go bump in the night!
A classic of innovative paper
engineering and beautifully
finished illustrations.
☆ 5-8

FANCY THAT
Jan Pienkowski
Orchard hbk £3.50
ISBN 1852133457

Remember the old lady
who swallowed a fly? Here's
the story in pop- up form,
delightful small sized ideas
for little hands.
4-6

The Most Amazing
Hide & Seek Book

Lucy Cousins

Lucy Cousins wrote and illustrated her first book when she was still a student! She studied at Canterbury Art College and at the famous Royal College of Art.

She uses vivid and striking colours and shapes that young children respond to very positively.

The Maisy books have made her famous in 13 countries (especially in Japan) and you can now buy Maisy posters, cards and stickers.

She is married and lives in Hampshire with her husband and two young children called Josie and Oliver (Za-za's Baby Brother is dedicated to them).

Some books by Lucy Cousins:

Maisy Goes to Bed
Maisy Goes Swimming
Maisy Goes to the Playground
Maisy's ABC
Maisy's House
Za-za's Baby Brother
Noah's Ark

(all published by Walker Books)

WHEELS ON THE BUS
Paul Zelinsky
Orchard hbk £8.50
ISBN 1852132728

A favourite song, graphically depicted in a book filled with moving parts.

5–8

Beware of Boys

Picture Books

These books will all be enjoyed as shared stories by pre-schoolers. Many of them will also be enjoyed independently by school children, so we have not specified age-bands.

EACH PEACH PEAR PLUM
Janet & Allan Ahlberg
Puffin pbk £4.99
ISBN 0140509194

Janet Ahlberg's untimely death in 1995 brought an end to children's publishing's best-loved husband and wife team. 'Each Peach Pear Plum' takes pre-school children on a delightful journey through popular nursery rhymes whilst playing 'I Spy'.

☆

PEEPO!
Janet & Allan Ahlberg
Puffin pbk £4.99
ISBN 0140503846

Highly recommended book in verse, showing baby's day from morning until night with the aid of a cut out peephole.

WHERE'S MY TEDDY?
Jez Alborough
Walker pbk £3.99

ISBN 074453058X

Rhythmic, rhyming story about the sudden panic of losing your teddy bear. Wonderful for sharing with three year olds, as well as for older children to read themselves.

THE LIGHTHOUSE KEEPER'S LUNCH
Rhonda & David Armitage
Scholastic pbk £3.99
ISBN 0590551752

A humorous story with lots of ingredients to amuse and entertain. The seagulls who steal the lighthouse keeper's lunch have cartoon type speech bubbles which children can read aloud.

☆

THOMAS THE TANK ENGINE
Reverend Awdry
Heinemann hbk £3.99
ISBN 0434927759

Reverend Awdry started this series 50 years ago and his son Christopher has proudly carried on the tradition, delighting yet another generation.

THE MOUSEHOLE CAT
Antonia Barber, illustrations Nicola Bayley
Walker Books pbk £4.99
ISBN 0744523532

Enchanting Cornish folk tale of Mowzer the cat and his master, Tom the fisherman, who save the village of Mousehole from the Great Storm Cat. Bewitching full page illustrations.

☆

THE PATCHWORK CAT
Nicola Bayley
Red Fox pbk £3.99
ISBN 0099983206

Tabby the cat loves her patchwork quilt. When her owners put it out with the rubbish she sets off to track it down. Bayley's charming story is illuminated by rich and detailed illustrations.

Did you Know?

Ruth Brown found school very dull. The only person she could relate to was her art teacher! Ruth trained as an artist but only thought of writing and illustrating children's books when her good friend Pat Hutchins suggested it.

PETER AND THE WOLF
Ian Beck
Corgi Pbk £3.95
ISBN 0552527556

A wonderful re-telling of Prokofiev's classic tale with jewel-bright pictures. Superb for family story-time, especially if it is read along with the music from the tape.

 ☆

Quentin Blake

Perhaps best known for his hilarious illustrations for many of Roald Dahl's books, Quentin Blake is also a best-selling author/illustrator in his own right.

MR MAGNOLIA
Collins pbk £3.99
ISBN 1856811921

Zany rhymes and illustrations abound in this great read-aloud book. Children will love the infectious rhythm of the text. If you don't like being asked to read the same book time and time again, then avoid this one!
☆

SIMPKIN
Red Fox pbk £4.50
ISBN 0099302306

Blake's hilarious illustrations bring to life this child's introduction to the world of opposites. Simple rhymes take us through Simpkin's day and his extremes of behaviour. A fun story to read aloud.

BEWARE OF BOYS
Tony Blundell
Puffin pbk £3.99
ISBN 014054156X

A highly entertaining reworking of the Big Bad Wolf stories in which a small boy outwits a wolf who captures him for dinner. Very amusing.

Raymond Briggs

Raymond Briggs is an accomplished author/illustrator who has the enviable talent of being able to write for children of all ages. He has won the Kate Greenaway Medal twice, for the Mother Goose Treasury (now out of print) and for 'Father Christmas', a story book with cartoon speech bubbles.

THE SNOWMAN
Puffin pbk £4.99
ISBN 0140503501

A timeless classic appealing to all ages. Wonderful illustrations and a warm-hearted story without any text. It is a perfect book for sharing at home.

WILLY THE WIMP
Anthony Browne
Walker pbk £4.99
ISBN 0744543630

The character Willy the Gorilla will be a winner with children who have experienced bullying at school. Willy decides to make some changes so that he can get the better

of his bullies, and he is soon no longer a wimp who is frightened of everything and everybody - or is he?

A DARK DARK TALE
Ruth Brown
Red Fox pbk £4.50
ISBN 0099874008

A jet-black cat steals her way deeper and deeper into a gloomy house and finally uncovers a mouse. A charming story with a recurring 'dark' motif, ideal for reading aloud.

Simpkin

MIFFY
Dick Bruna
Mammoth pbk £3.99
ISBN 0416506402

Bruna's wonderful bold drawings and bright colours make Miffy the Rabbit easily identifiable to toddlers.

John Burningham

John Burningham's award-winning success can be attributed to two things in particular; his subtle and memorable use of pencil illustrations, and his innovative use of text.

GRANPA
Puffin pbk £3.99
ISBN 0140508414

Granpa is the profoundly moving story of a little girl's stay with, and subsequent loss of her grandparent. Burningham conveys a sense of affectionate memory and sorrow without ever becoming morbid or over-sentimental. ☆

OI! GET OFF OUR TRAIN
Red Fox pbk £4.99
ISBN 009985340X

A sleeping boy dreams of driving a train, aided by his loyal pyjama-case dog. On their travels the duo rescue and befriend many endangered animals. A touching tale with an environmental theme.

WHERE'S JULIUS?
Red Fox pbk £4.99
ISBN 0099200716

Julius lives in a world of his own and his parents must travel to Egypt, Africa and Russia to bring him his meals. A charming homage to the power of the child's imagination.

Nick Butterworth

Nick Butterworth began as a graphic designer before moving into children's books. His illustrations are renowned for their crisp, clear quality and their close links to the well-written text. Best known for his popular Percy the Park-Keeper books, he has also written and illustrated books for toddlers.

JASPER'S BEANSTALK
Illustrations Mick Inkpen
Hodder pbk £3.99
ISBN 0340586346

Jasper the cat sets out to grow a beanstalk, carefully tending to his planted bean every day. An enchanting tale in this popular Jasper series with strong colourful pictures and large, clear print.

ONE SNOWY NIGHT
Collins pbk £4.50
ISBN 0006643183

One winter's night, Percy rescues his animal friends from the cold in the first book of the series. Butterworth's illustrations are exquisitely detailed and full of gentle humour. 🗨

DEAR ZOO
Rod Campbell
Puffin pbk £4.99
ISBN 014050446X

A simple story about the search for a pet. Lift the flaps to uncover each exotic but unsuitable animal the zoo sends. A wonderful book for introducing animal words to small children.
Hbk from Campbell Books

Miffy

The Very Hungry Caterpillar

FARMYARD TALES
**Stephen Cartwright &
Heather Amery**
Usborne pbk £2.50 – £2.95

The day-to-day adventures
of Mrs Boot the farmer and
her children Poppy and Sam
form the basis for a series of
delightful stories with simple,
short texts and lovely,
detailed pictures.

Babette Cole

*Babette Cole was born in
the Channel Islands and
now lives in Kent with an
assortment of pets and farm
animals. She worked as a
writer and illustrator after
graduating from art school.
Children's books are her passion
and her works are full of
energy and humour.*

THE TROUBLE WITH MUM
Mammoth pbk £3.99
ISBN 0749710209

This mum is a little different
to other mums- she's a witch.
No-one accepts her until the
day the school is ablaze and
she saves the day with her
magic rain spell. One of the
wonderfully entertaining
'The Trouble With' series.

THE VERY HUNGRY
CATERPILLAR
Eric Carle
Puffin pbk £4.50
ISBN 0140500871

This is the story of a small
hungry caterpillar who eats
his way through a variety
of different foods before
turning into a beautiful
butterfly. A charming
picture book which is also
an excellent way to introduce children to counting.

PRINCESS SMARTYPANTS
Collins pbk £4.50
ISBN 0006627986

Great illustrations, great story. A twist on the old princess-must-marry-a-prince theme. This princess knows what's what and stays happily unmarried in the company of her pets. A memorable anti-stereotype and a very funny story.

THE BEAR UNDER THE STAIRS
Helen Cooper
Corgi pbk £3.99
ISBN 0552527068

More than just a useful tale in helping children overcome fears of dark spaces this book has rich, magical illustrations and a wonderful sense of humour.

Noah's Ark

NOAH'S ARK
Retold and illustrated by Lucy Cousins
Walker pbk £4.99
ISBN 0744536723

A vibrant and cheerful approach to a popular Old Testament story. A clear and simple text and illustration leave lots of scope for children to add their own narrative (and animal noises!)

RAINFOREST
Helen Cowcher
Corgi pbk £3.99
ISBN 0552525537

Cowcher's beautifully stylised drawings evoke a very real atmosphere of rainforest humidity and excitement. She uses few words but does her story-telling through illustration. An attractive introduction to environmental awareness for children.

HAIRY MACLARY FROM DONALDSON'S DAIRY
Lynley Dodd
Puffin pbk £3.99
ISBN 0140505318

The first in a series featuring the scruffy dog and his friends all of whom have equally catchy names. Children love the rhyme, repetition and rhythm of these best-selling stories.

DINOSAURS AND ALL THAT RUBBISH
Michael Foreman
Puffin pbk £4.99
ISBN 014055260X

First published in 1972, this book raises issues which are now familiar, yet were unusual for a children's book at the time of publication. When Man decides to explore a distant star, he leaves the Earth in a terrible mess. He can only return to earth if he learns to care for it. A book for any child who takes an interest in the world around them.

MR LITTLE'S NOISY BOAT
Richard Fowler
Mammoth pbk £3.99
ISBN 0749710276

One of Richard Fowler's brilliant lift-the-flap series. A wacky storyline and informative illustrations combine to make these books favourites.

Princess Smartypants

Rod Campbell

Rod Campbell was born in Scotland and brought up in Rhodesia. Although he is now an artist, he actually graduated from University with a PhD in Organic Chemistry!

His first children's book was published in 1980 and soon after followed the ever-popular 'Dear Zoo'. He has produced almost 100 books for the under 5's and all have a learning bias with flaps and tabs and other innovative elements.

Rod Campbell now lives in France.

His other books include:

My Presents   **Buster's Day**
It's Mine!   *(all published by Macmillan)*
Oh Dear!

OLIVER'S VEGETABLES
Vivian French
& Alison Bartlett
Hodder pbk £4.99
ISBN 0340634790

An original and strikingly visual story about a boy who will only eat chips. One day he goes to stay with his grandparents, and discovers how much he enjoys vegetables.

JAMAICA'S FIND
Juanita Havill
Mammoth pbk £3.50
ISBN 0749701900

Jamaica finds a red woolly hat and a cuddly toy dog whilst out playing. She hands the hat into the lost property office, but is reluctant to surrender the dog. An engaging morality tale.

EAT UP GEMMA
Sarah Hayes
Walker pbk £3.99
ISBN 0744513286

A humorous look at the all-too-familiar traumas of mealtimes and the attempts of Gemma's family to get her to finish her meals.

KATIE MORAG AND THE TWO GRANDMOTHERS
Mairi Hedderwick
Collins pbk £3.99
ISBN 000664273X

Granny Island's prize sheep needs a drastic makeover. Granny Mainland solves the problem in a unexpected way. Katie Morag, the wee scamp from the Isle of Struay never fails to delight.

WHERE'S SPOT?
Eric Hill
Puffin pbk £4.50
ISBN 0140506500

Where's Spot? is a wonderful beginning to your child's reading. An early learning classic, it has flaps to lift on every page and satisfies the most inquisitive mind.

OLD BEAR
Jane Hissey
Red Fox pbk £3.99
ISBN 0099554402

Old Bear and his friends need little introduction. Jane Hissey's characters have been made into very popular television characters. The books of Old Bear, Bramwell Brown, Rabbit, Monkey and the others will delight children with their lifelike illustrations.

Oliver's Vedgetables

Did you Know?

Jane Hissey seeks inspiration from her childhood toys and if you were to peek inside her toy box you would see Old Bear and Jolly Tall

Shirley Hughes

Shirley Hughes is a well-loved author for 3-5 year olds. She tells stories easily recognised by a toddler and has a very distinctive style of illustration.

DOGGER
Red Fox pbk £3.99
ISBN 009992790X

The heartbreaking story of Dave and his beloved toy which is lost and then retrieved. Hughes hits the spot with childhood anxieties. ☆

ALFIE'S FEET
Red Fox pbk £3.50
ISBN 0099922401

Alfie is a wonderful first hero whose antics with his new shoes are familiar and funny. Little sister Annie Rose is a great side-kick.

Pat Hutchins

Rosie's Walk appeared in 1969, in the week in which Pat Hutchins' first son was born. Her unique style of illustrating with its use of vibrant colours and incredible detail have made her an evergreen author/illustrator.

ROSIE'S WALK
Puffin pbk £3.99
ISBN 0140500324

An enjoyable and amusing story about a hen who takes a walk and unwittingly leads a fox who is following her into one disaster after another. A perfect first book.

CLOCKS AND MORE CLOCKS
Puffin pbk £3.99
ISBN 014050091X

The colourful central character, Mr Higgins, finds a clock in his attic. He then buys another and another, because he cannot understand why the clocks all have different times. Wonderful stylized artwork.

Mick Inkpen

Since entering the world of children's books in 1987 Mick Inkpen has firmly established himself as one of its foremost author/illustrators. The wit and warmth of his illustrations coupled with the comical antics and charm of characters such as Kipper, Penguin Small and Threadbear have made him a favourite with children.

KIPPER'S TOYBOX
Hodder pbk £3.99
ISBN 0340580496

Fearing for the safety of his much loved toys, Kipper is determined to discover who or what has been nibbling his toy box. Every child will empathise with Kipper as he double-checks that none of his toys is missing.

Clocks and More Clocks

PENGUIN SMALL

Hodder pbk £5.99
ISBN 034061935X

When the penguins leave the North Pole to escape the bullying polar bears, non-swimming Penguin Small gets left behind. An enchanting story of friendship and adventure with Mick Inkpen's customary wealth of images and fabulous illustrations.

THREADBEAR

Hodder pbk £4.99
ISBN 0340573503

There is only one thing that has always been wrong with Threadbear – in his tummy is a squeaker that has never squeaked. However, with a little help from Father Christmas (and a trip to the land where the squeaker tree grows), he is soon on the road to recovery.

DEAR GREENPEACE

Simon James
Walker Books pbk £3.99
ISBN 0744530601

The story is told in letters written to Greenpeace about a whale in the garden pond. Full of imagination and humour, with clear illustrations which will appeal to the under fives.

It was Jake

THE DAY JAKE VACUUMED

Simon James
Macmillan pbk £3.99
ISBN 0330312499

Mischievous Jake is larger than life in this funny, colourful story about helping around the house (or not, as the case may be).

IT WAS JAKE

Anita Jeram
Walker Books pbk £3.99
ISBN 0744523109

Poor old Jake, Danny's canine buddy, gets the blame for everything - the mess, the noise, the trouble, until Danny's mum works out who the mischief-maker really is.

THE TIGER WHO CAME TO TEA

Judith Kerr
Collins pbk £4.50
ISBN 0006640613

For over 20 years children have been enthralled and delighted by this fanciful tale of a tiger joining a little girl and her mum for tea one day. Funny and entertaining.

MOG THE FORGETFUL CAT

Judith Kerr
Collins pbk £4.50
ISBN 0006640621

Mog is the kind of cat children everywhere will love. She's big, fat and forgetful and is a nuisance around the house till one day she surprises everyone by inadvertently stopping a burglar.

Nick Butterworth
& Mick Inkpen

Both hugely popular in their own rights, Mick and Nick actually started out together in a graphic design studio in London designing greetings cards, cartoon strips and the packaging of Loveable Bras!

Mick Inkpen is the creator of Kipper, who has probably superseded Spot now as the most cuddly dog in picture books! His first solo book was 'One Bear at Bedtime' which is still a bestseller for Hodder and his most recent is 'Nothing', a 1995 Christmas bestseller.

Mick Inkpen says 'Without the experience of having children, I doubt whether I would have been capable of producing a good children's book'.

Nick Butterworth grew up in his parents' sweet shop in Essex (every child's dream!). His Percy the Park Keeper books are phenomenally successful and his latest book 'A Year in Percy's Park' is a stunning compilation of these four books. Child Education has called Nick 'a real friend to small children'.

Some books by Mick:
Penguin Small
Kipper
The Blue Balloon
Lullabyhullaballoo
Threadbear
Wibbly Pig
(all published by Hodder Children's Books)

Some books by Nick:
One Snowy Night
The Rescue Party
After the Storm
The Secret Path
The Fox's Hiccups
The Cross Rabbit
(all published by Collins Children's Books)

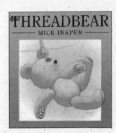 

WHEN SHEEP CANNOT SLEEP - The Counting Book
Satoshi Kitamura
Red Fox pbk £3.99
ISBN 0099505401

Kitamura has a distinctive and quirky style and this book is no exception. An original and beautifully illustrated counting story which stimulates readers' visual, verbal and numeric skills.

☆

ELMER
David McKee
Red Fox pbk £4.50
ISBN 0099697203

Elmer the patchwork elephant loves playing tricks on his fellow elephants. McKee achieves his striking look with bright, simple colours and a bold sense of fun.

NOT NOW BERNARD
David McKee
Red Fox pbk £4.50
ISBN 0099240505

There's a real sting in this tale when trusting Bernard gets eaten by a monster, much to his parents' indifference. Recommended reading for those who believe children should be seen and not heard!

THE MAN WHOSE MOTHER WAS A PIRATE
Margaret Mahy, illustrated Margaret Chamberlain
Puffin pbk £3.99
ISBN 0140506241

The off-beat and original tale of the little man, Sam, and his pirate mother who against all good advice travel with a wheelbarrow and a kite to see the sea. Vibrantly illustrated.

SIX DINNER SID
Inga Moore
Macdonald pbk £3.99
ISBN 0750003049

Sid is a six-dinners-a-day kind of cat. Therefore he lives not only at number 1 Aristotle Street, but at numbers, 2, 3, 4, 5 and 6 as well! None of his six owners are aware of this as they don't talk to each other, but one day they find out!

THE PAPER BAG PRINCESS
Robert N Munsch
Scholastic pbk £2.99
ISBN 0590711261

Princess Elizabeth's perfect world is shattered when a dragon burns her clothes and steals away her fiancé, Prince Ronald. She outwits the dragon and finds her prince with unexpected consequences. Very funny.

ON THE WAY HOME
Jill Murphy
Macmillan pbk £3.99
ISBN 0333375726

Claire has fallen and bumped her knee. On the way home she tells all sorts of tales about how it happened, but the reader must guess which one is true.

ALL IN ONE PIECE
Jill Murphy
Macmillan pbk £3.99
ISBN 0744509335

Mr and Mrs Large are trying to get ready for the office dinner dance. Their four mischievous elephant childre however, are making it very difficult for them to get out of the house in one piece. Murphy provides a warm an humorous portrayal of famil life, instantly appealing to children as well as to parent who may find the situation strangely familiar!

MEG AND MOG
Helen Nicoll & Jan Pienkowski
Puffin pbk £3.99

Meg and Mog

ISBN 0140501177

Since the early 1970's the antics of inept witch, Meg and her cat, Mog, have provided bewitching entertainment. The books, in bold colour, encourage an affection for the characters whilst maintaining the fascination of children for all things witch-like.

David McKee

David McKee was born and brought up in South Devon. Before he turned to children's books he drew cartoons for 'Punch', 'Times Educational Children's Supplement' and 'Reader's Digest'.

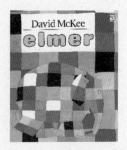

His first book was published in 1964 and the very popular Mr Benn (later made into a TV series) appeared in 1971. Mr Benn still has fan clubs in Universities today!

The surreal elements of his illustration jolt children into paying attention and usually into laughter. Books for Keeps called his work 'as thought-provoking for adults as it is amusing for children'.

'Not Now Bernard', now a National Curriculum title is possibly his most surreal title and famous for its rather grisly ending.

Some other books by David McKee:

The Sad Story of Veronica Who Played the Violin
The Snow Woman
The Monster and the Teddy Bear
Tusk Tusk

David McKee is probably best known now for his colourful and humorous Elmer stories.
(all published by Red Fox)

THE COMPLETE TALES OF BEATRIX POTTER
Frederick Warne hbk £35.00
ISBN 0723236186

Beatrix Potter's 23 tales and verses are brought together in one large format volume, complete with her original enchanting illustrations. Arranged in the same order as they were published, and with an introductory note which connects the real places, people and animals in her life with those in each story, this is the perfect gift for any Potter fan.

WINNIE THE WITCH
Korky Paul & Valerie Thomas
Oxford UP pbk £2.99
ISBN 0192721976

A winner of the Children's Book Award, this zanily illustrated tale charts the domestic problems (and their resolution) of Winnie and her cat. A great story, promoting friendship and tolerance.

WE'RE GOING ON A BEAR HUNT
Michael Rosen,
illustrations Helen Oxenbury
Walker Books pbk £3.99
ISBN 0744523230

A classic picture book for under-sevens, demanding participation from its audience. "Swishy-swashy! Splasy-splosh! Hoo Woo!" bellows Rosen's loud and boisterous text.
Its wonderful rhythm encourages you to join in. Add to this Oxenbury's lively watercolours and you have a classic in the making.

☆

DON'T DO THAT!
Tony Ross
Red Fox pbk £3.99
ISBN 0099917106

Nellie has a very pretty nose. A nose so pretty that it wins pretty nose competitions. Then one day she does the unmentionable and her finger is firmly stuck up there! Absurd attempts to remove it follow with everyone from the local farmer to a scientist trying but failing. Inventive and full of grotesque humour that children will cherish.

I WANT TO BE
Tony Ross
Collins pbk £4.99
ISBN 0006643574

No one can fail to be enchanted by the little Princess who is wondering how to be grown up. Eventually the maid offers the best advice. A story that succeeds in suggesting what is good and right in a humorous way and without moralising.

Winnie the Witch

THE TRUE STORY OF THE THREE LITTLE PIGS
Jon Scieszka, illustrations Lane Smith
Puffin pbk £3.99
ISBN 0140540563

Superbly illustrated, this is the big bad wolf's version of the classic tale. He thinks he got a rough deal and tells you so in spoof Chandler style. Smith's illustrations are a rich dark combination of oils and collage which create a wonderful playground for the imagination.

WHERE THE WILD THINGS ARE
Maurice Sendak
Collins pbk £4.99
ISBN 0006640869

'Where the Wild Things Are' tells the story of Max, who tames the wild things at night when he puts on his wolf suit and sails off in his boat. A reassuring story about how to overcome night fears, this is an award-winning, acknowledged children's classic.
☆

THE WHALE'S SONG
Dyan Sheldon, illustrations Gary Blythe
Red Fox pbk £4.50
ISBN 0099737604

Lily believes her Grandmother's stories of the whales' singing, and one magical evening hears them for herself. A beautifully illustrated and atmospheric tale capturing the wonder of nature.
☆

JANINE AND THE NEW BABY
Iolette Thomas
Mammoth pbk £3.50
ISBN 0749706511

Janine would have liked a pet rabbit better than a new baby, but by the end of this story all her questions are answered and her fears assuaged.

THE THREE LITTLE WOLVES & THE BIG BAD PIG
Eugene Trivizas, illustrations Helen Oxenbury
Mammoth pbk £3.99
ISBN 0749725052

A wonderfully comic re-telling of the tale of the Three Little Pigs introducing new houses of concrete, plexiglas and...flowers! Enchanting illustrations.

Where the Wild Things Are

BADGER'S PARTING GIFTS
Susan Varley
Collins pbk £4.50
ISBN 0006643175

Recommended by the
Pre-School Playgroup
Association, this moving
story helps children to come
to terms with the death of a
loved one by treasuring
their memories.

THE ELEPHANT AND THE BAD BABY
Elfrida Vipont
Puffin pbk £3.99
ISBN 0140500480

An elephant goes out for a
walk and meets a bad baby.
They embark on a
'rumpeting' run through
town and one by one various
members of the town give
chase. Vipont uses rhythmic
repetition in the best tradition of 'The Gingerbread
Man' and 'The Enormous
Turnip', making this a fun
story to read aloud.

CAN'T YOU SLEEP, LITTLE BEAR?
Martin Waddell,
illustrations Barbara Firth
Walker pbk £3.99
ISBN 0744513162

Waddell has created a
loveable, insomniac little
bear that many will appreciate.
A book that has become a
classic, not least for its beautifully soothing illustrations.
☆

FARMER DUCK
Martin Waddell,
illustrations Helen Oxenbury
Walker pbk £4.50
ISBN 074453660X

The lazy farmer lounges
in bed all day munching
chocolate whilst down-trodden
duck gets to do all the hard
work - that is until the other
animals hatch a plot to send
him packing. Oxenbury's
larger-than-life illustrations
are glorious.
☆

THE TUNNEL
Brian Wildsmith
Oxford pbk £3.99
ISBN 0192722883

Wildsmith has written a
topical travel book in French
& English. It's about two
moles who dig under the
channel and meet with each
other in the middle. The
collage-style illustrations are
unusual and colourful.

THE VELVETEEN RABBIT
Margery Williams
Mammoth pbk £3.99
ISBN 0749710551

The tale of the Velveteen
Rabbit's life in the Nursery
and his quest to become
'real'; the funny, sometimes
sad, but always magical story
of life as seen through the
toy's eyes.

DR XARGLE'S BOOK OF EARTHLETS
Jeanne Willis,
illustrations Tony Ross
Red Fox pbk £3.99
ISBN 0099640104

Dr Xargle teaches his class
of aliens about the weird
and wonderful world of
'earthlets' (aka human
babies). Zany and rib-tickling,
this is one in a series of
studies of all things strange
from Earth.

BUT WHERE IS THE GREEN PARROT?
Thomas & Wanda Zacharias
Macmillan pbk £3.50
ISBN 0330303554

An excellent, interactive
book with a green parrot
hidden in every picture. A
superb way to persuade really
small children to concen-
trate on the page in front
of them.

The Elephant and the Bad Baby

Martin Waddell

Some of Martin
Waddell's books;
**Can't You Sleep
Little Bear?**
The Park in the Dark
Once There Were Giants
The Hidden House
Rosie's Babies
Let's Go Home Little Bear
Farmer Duck
Owl Babies

(All published by Walker Books)

Martin Waddell went to London to play for Fulham FC's junior team when he was 15! After a year he decided to fall back on his second great love which is writing and after 10 years he moved back to his current home in Newcastle, County Down, Northern Ireland - a stone's throw from where he lived as a boy during the war.

Martin writes picture books, books for first readers and also books for teenagers - some of them under the pseudonym Catherine Sefton. His most famous book is probably the bedtime story 'Can't You Sleep, Little Bear' which was inspired by his experiences with his own children.

His books have won many awards including the Smarties, the Kate Greenaway and the Kurt Maschler.

His strengths lie in his ability as a storyteller, his control of his material, his gentle humour, and his understanding of the child's mind

'You need a big emotion at the centre of a picture book, that a child can identify with...'

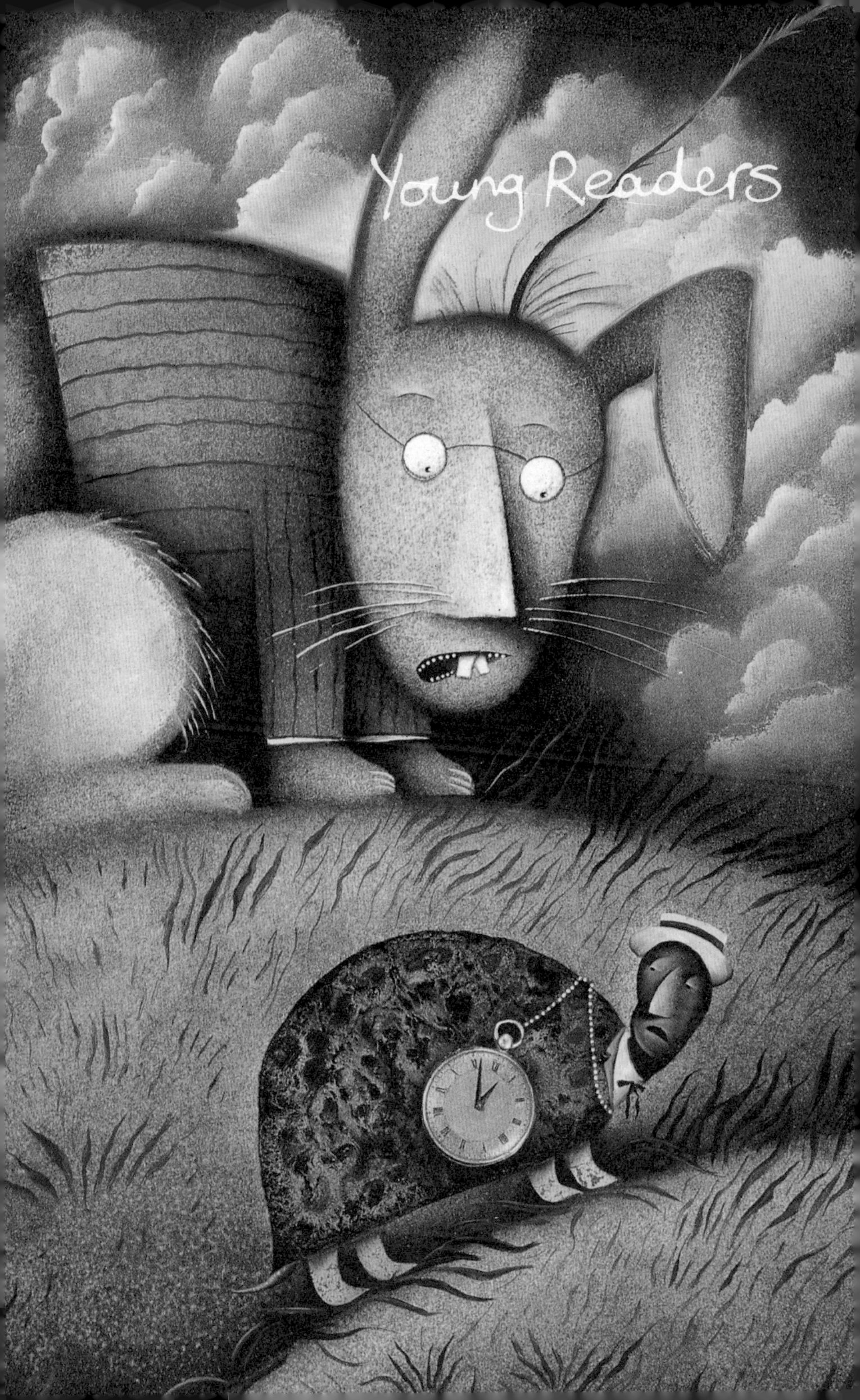
Young Readers

Young Readers

This is such an exciting time in a child's reading life. They are beginning to read by themselves and therefore discovering the wonder of becoming lost in a book.

Although reading will be a daily part of their school lives, continuing to read at home is an equally important part of children's education as it not only improves their reading skills but is also a reminder that books are a source of pleasure and not just a school activity.

In our book selection we have remembered that reading ability at this age is variable. The books range from picture books and reading series right through to more complex story books. We recommend that you also revisit picture books from the pre-school selection. A familiar story is often a great confidence booster when reading alone for the first time.

Children of this age often enjoy funny stories and books that expand their sense of reality with witches, magic and fantastic scenarios. We have also chosen books that incorporate good illustrations into text. This breaks up the story and increases interest in the characters.

There is a whole new world of authors and characters to discover when you learn to read. Dr Seuss, Paddington, My Naughty Little Sister, The Worst Witch and so many more are all here. Read on...

Mummy Laid an Egg
Previous page:
The Stinky Cheeseman

Picture Books for 5-8 Year Olds

Just because children have started reading by themselves it doesn't mean that they can't still enjoy picture books. In fact, they are an excellent way of adding confidence in reading as the format is still familiar. Here we have chosen a few exceptional picture books with more text, that children can try their new reading skills out on.

JIM AND THE BEANSTALK
Raymond Briggs
Puffin pbk £4.99
ISBN 0140500774

An hilarious variation on the Jack and the Beanstalk tale in which Jim climbs the beanstalk to find a harmless, bald, toothless and short-sighted giant. Full of Briggs' unique humour with a delicious twist at the end.

BROTHER EAGLE SISTER SKY
Chief Seattle,
illustrations Susan Jeffers
Puffin pbk £4.99
ISBN 014054514X

Nearly 150 years ago, Chief Seattle, a respected and peaceful leader of one of the North West Indian Nations, delivered a compelling speech warning of the dangers of destroying nature for future generations. Susan Jeffers' beautiful illustrations bring his words to life, creating a moving and powerful plea for conservation.

MUMMY LAID AN EGG
Babette Cole
Red Fox pbk £4.50
ISBN 0099299119

When Mum and Dad try and tell the kids about the birds and the bees they get it all wrong. Luckily, their clever children set them straight. This hilarious guide to the facts of life is frank, factual and a good introduction for parents!

THE ENORMOUS CROCODILE
Roald Dahl, illustrations Quentin Blake
Puffin pbk £4.99
ISBN 0140503420

A marvellous tale about a big bad crocodile who wants to eat 'juicy' and 'yummy' children for lunch but is foiled by the ingenious animals in the jungle. The witty text is complemented by the funny illustrations.

THE GIRAFFE, THE PELLY AND ME
Roald Dahl, illustrations Quentin Blake
Puffin pbk £4.50
ISBN 0140505660

The enthralling tale of the Ladderless Window Cleaning Company (giraffe, pelican and monkey) and their friend Billy, who together embark on the job of a lifetime: cleaning all 677 windows of the Duke of Hampshire's house, with spectacularly funny results.

THE PATCHWORK QUILT
Valerie Flournoy
Puffin pbk £4.99
ISBN 0140554335

A gentle, touching book which follows the making of Grandma's quilt and all the memories it contains. A warm and accessible celebration of family life and history.

SCHOOL
Colin & Jacqui Hawkins
Collins pbk £4.50
ISBN 0006645674

Watch out teachers, bullies and creeps – here is the Hawkins' definitive guide to life within the school gates. An outrageously irreverent look at school life for school kids of all ages.

AMAZING GRACE
Mary Hoffman
Frances Lincoln pbk £3.99
ISBN 0711206996

Grace has a wonderfully wild imagination and loves to act out stories and dress up.

JOLLY ROGER
Colin McNaughton
Walker pbk £4.99
ISBN 074451732X

Roger becomes a cabin-boy on a pirate ship and embarks upon a rumbustious romp

book should be: the Little Red Hen curses the ISBN and Chicken Licken is squashed by the table of contents!

THE CHOCOLATE WEDDING
Posy Simmonds
Puffin pbk £3.99
ISBN 014054531X

Too ill to be a bridesmaid, Lulu goes on an

How Dogs Really Work

When she wants to be Peter Pan in the school play and some of the other children try to discourage her, Ma and Grandma show her that she can be anything she wants to be.

BULLY
David Hughes
Walker pbk £4.99
ISBN 0744536243

A powerful exploration of playground bullying which tackles the problem in a bold, blunt yet accessible manner.

☆

across the high seas. This is an energetic cruise through pirate life, filled with jokes, curses and lots of yo-ho-hos!

☆

THE STINKY CHEESEMAN AND OTHER FAIRLY STUPID TALES
Jon Scieszka, illustrations Lane Smith
Puffin pbk £4.99
ISBN 0140548963

Full of wild creatures, bizarre ideas, mad typography and surreal images, this reworking of old fashioned fairy tales is a classic. It stretches the barriers of what a picture

amazing voyage on a chocolate sea, outwits chocolate mice and rescues the sugar bride. Simmonds' detailed cartoon strip illustrations tell a lively and memorable cautionary tale of over-indulgence.

HOW DOGS REALLY WORK
Alan Snow
Collins pbk £4.99
ISBN 0006643191

A unique 'owner's manual' complete with inside mechanics, family tree and tips for general maintenance. This off-the-wall guide is a must for all dog lovers. Also available in mini format.

DON QUIXOTE
Marcia Williams
Walker pbk £3.99
ISBN 0744536251

A unique and superbly illustrated retelling of the famous story. Williams' humorous cartoon style makes this version instantly and amusingly accessible.

Reading Series for Young Readers

The good thing about books in a reading series is that you can be sure they will all have a consistent level of language and vocabulary, even if they are by different authors. The series below have been selected because they offer support to first readers without sacrificing interest and style.

FAVOURITE TALES
Ladybird hbk £1.25 each

Over 30 popular fairy tales in attractive and affordable individual volumes. Consistent, easy-to-read texts and bright illustrations

throughout. Titles include 'The Sleeping Beauty', 'Cinderella' and many others.

HAPPY FAMILIES
Allan Ahlberg
Puffin pbk £3.25 each

A series of individual stories, ideal for bridging the gap between picture books and early readers. Based on the updated (more PC) characters from the card game, each story is full of slapstick humour set in identifiable and reassuring situations. Titles include 'Miss Jump the Jockey' and 'Mr Biff the Boxer'.

JETS
Collins pbk £2.99 each

Lively stories with integral black and white illustrations, suitable for children gaining in reading confidence. Watch out especially for the Bob Wilson, Rose Impey and Colin West titles. Children can then move on to 'Jumbo Jets' which are similar in style to Jets but with longer texts for more confident and accomplished readers.

I CAN READ
Mammoth pbk £3.99 each

A gentle beginner reader series with large, well-spaced type and simple, colour illustrations. Else Minarik's irresistible Little Bear (with great Sendak illustrations)

and Arnold Lobel's buoyant, decisive Frog and endearingly slow Toad are particular favourites.

RED NOSE READERS
Allan Ahlberg and Colin McNaughton
Walker Books pbk £2.50 each

A subversively comic first reading scheme arranged in three levels. Deceptively simple texts, illustrated in full colour with textual and visual jokes and puns.

SPRINTERS
Walker Books pbk £2.99 each

A series written by very well known authors like Brian Patten and Dick King-Smith, aimed at making the first big step from picture books. While they look like 'proper' books, they are encouragingly full of illustrations and short chapters.

BEGINNER BOOKS
Dr Seuss
Collins pbk £3.50 each

Dr Seuss's ridiculous rhymes and absurd characters are a brilliant introduction to the richness of language. The illustrations are wacky and children love the zany humour. The best titles include 'Green Eggs and Ham', 'Hop on Pop', and the well-loved 'The Cat in the Hat'.

Terence Blacker

Terence Blacker has a wife, two children, five chickens, three cats, one guinea pig and a rat!

When he was young he wanted to be a champion jockey at steeplechasing but instead he worked in publishing and now is a well known writer - especially for his Ms Wiz books (there are now 10 of them). His worst memory is being described by his headmaster as 'the most disobedient boy in the school!'

His best review was

"I am dyslexic and I find reading very difficult. I started reading your books and I found them very interesting and funny. I did not enjoy books before."

Reader in St Albans

His worst review was

'This book is extremely silly and unfunny'

School Librarian

Some Books by Terence Blacker;
**Ms Wiz Smells Trouble
In Stitches Ms Wiz
You're Nicked Ms Wiz
In Control Ms Wiz
Ms Wiz Goes Live**

(all published by Macmillan)

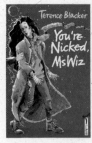

First Story Books for 5-8 Year Olds

IT WAS A DARK AND STORMY NIGHT
Janet & Allan Ahlberg
Puffin pbk £4.99
ISBN 0140545867

Antonio is kidnapped and forced to entertain his captors by telling them stories. The bandits won't be satisfied however, and they argue so much about the plots that Antonio manages to slip quietly home.

JEREMIAH IN THE DARK WOODS
Janet & Allan Ahlberg
Puffin pbk £3.99
ISBN 0140328114

Jeremiah Obadiah Jackanory Jones goes in search of the thief who stole his grandmother's tarts and encounters several storybook characters in a tongue-in-cheek look at traditional stories.

THE RAILWAY CAT
Phyllis Arkle
Puffin pbk £3.25
ISBN 0140316604

Hack, the new railway porter, doesn't like cats and has plans to get rid of Alfie, the railway cat. Alfie's fight back is funny and action-packed.

SIMON AND THE WITCH
Margaret Stuart Barry
Collins pbk £2.99
ISBN 006720641

Is Simon's best friend really a witch? She is certainly cantankerous enough. Just wait until Simon begins to learn a few spells too!

MS WIZ SPELLS TROUBLE
Terence Blacker
Macmillan pbk £2.50
ISBN 0330310968

When feminist witch Ms Wiz takes over Class Three, strange things start to happen which have outrageously comic results.

HURRICANE BETSY
Malorie Blackman
Mammoth pbk £2.99
ISBN 0749714239

There are explosively funny results when Betsy decides to pre-empt the approaching hurricane with her own kind of storm. A lively story set in an evocative Caribbean background.

FRECKLE JUICE
Judy Blume
Macmillan pbk £2.50
ISBN 0330308297

Andrew wants freckles just like Nicky Lane, so his mum can't spot if he has a grubby neck! Freckle Juice seems the only solution – but what will really happen if he drinks it ...?

PADDINGTON
Michael Bond
Collins pbk £3.50
ISBN 000670428X

The classic story of the marmalade-eating bear who gets into endless embarrassing scrapes.

DILLY THE DINOSAUR
Tony Bradman
Mammoth pbk £2.99
ISBN 0749703660

The first book about Dilly, the naughtiest dinosaur in the world who gets even naughtier when he doesn't get his own way.

It was a Dark and Stormy Night

Flat Stanley

FLAT STANLEY
Jeff Brown, illustrations
Tomi Ungerer
Mammoth pbk £2.99
ISBN 0749701374

Stanley Lambchop suddenly
finds himself an inch thick
when a bulletin board falls
on him. This leads to endless
possibilities – squeezing
under doors, being posted
in envelopes and slipping
down drains. Illustrated
amusingly throughout.
⟦❝❞⟧

THE JULIAN STORIES
Ann Cameron
Transworld pbk £2.99
ISBN 0440863333

A collection of six lively
tales in which Julian gets
into plenty of mischief, and
explores the trials and
tribulations of family life
and childhood friendship.

MR MAJEIKA
Humphrey Carpenter
Puffin pbk £3.50
ISBN 0140316779

The first in a series of books
about the teacher with the
flying carpet and his magic
ways of dealing with trouble
makers. A fun and entertaining book for children who
have developed confidence
and reading fluency.

SAM THE GIRL DETECTIVE
Tony Bradman
Mammoth pbk £2.99
ISBN 0440862124

Introducing Sam Marlowe,
intrepid girl detective and
super sleuth par excellence.
These spoof thrillers have
funny, fast-moving plots
which will keep even the
most reluctant reader
turning the page.

MILLY-MOLLY-MANDY
Joyce Lankester Brisley
Puffin pbk £3.50
ISBN 0140305238

The book about the girl
with the short hair, short
legs and short frocks! Well-
loved and still absolutely
delightful, her traditional
and charming adventures
have been enjoyed since
the 1920's.

THE BIG ... SERIES
Rob Childs
Transworld pbk £2.50

An action-packed series following the adventures of two football-mad brothers. You don't have to be a football fan to enjoy these realistic and fast moving stories full of sporting action.

A DRAGON IN CLASS FOUR
June Counsel
Transworld pbk £2.50
ISBN 0440862671

When Scales, the dragon, joins Sam in Class 4, funny events begin to happen – especially as Scales can be seen by everyone but the teacher. The first in a fantasy series.

A GIFT FROM WINKLESEA
Helen Cresswell
Puffin pbk £3.25
ISBN 0140304932

Dan and his sister Mary find the ideal present for their mother at the seaside. The egg-shaped stone sits proudly on the mantelpiece until it hatches the Gift – and plenty of fun ensues.

THE MAGIC FINGER
Roald Dahl
Puffin pbk £3.50
ISBN 0140341625

The delightful tale of one girl's magic finger and the punishment it can deliver to those who make her angry. Wittily told and with a strong environmental theme.

FANTASTIC MR FOX
Roald Dahl
Puffin pbk £3.50
ISBN 0140326715

Mr Fox outwits the mean farmers Bunce, Boggis and Bean, with traditional Dahl flair. An action-filled adventure full of subversive humour.

AMBER BROWN IS NOT A CRAYON
Paula Danziger
Macmillan pbk £2.99
ISBN 0330331434

Amber's best friend Daniel is moving to a new town and they both have to work out how to cope with changes. An imaginative book full of gentle humour and observation.

MY NAUGHTY LITTLE SISTER
Dorothy Edwards
Mammoth pbk £2.99
ISBN 0749700548

Classic stories of the spirited, naughty little sister and her cohort Bad Harry. A gentle and reassuring look at misbehaviour.

The Magic Finger

Bill's New Frock

Readers who enjoyed the jokes of Pat Hutchins' book will be glad to discover she has written for older children too.

RATS
Pat Hutchins
Red Fox pbk £2.99
ISBN 0099931907

Sam wants a rat but his parents are against the idea. Eventually Nibbles joins the household and pandemonium is let loose, until something happens which makes Sam see Nibbles in a radically new light!

BILL'S NEW FROCK
Anne Fine
Mammoth pbk £2.99
ISBN 0582095565

Bill Simpson wakes up one morning to find out that he is a girl and is forced to go to school in a frilly pink dress. A brilliant and funny observation of the differences between boys and girls.

☆

THE SHRINKING OF TREEHORN
Florence Parry Heide
Puffin pbk £2.99
ISBN 014030746X

Treehorn is shrinking but adults just don't seem to notice, so he must save himself without their help. Wonderfully deadpan in tone, this is a classic comedy of adult-child relationships and can be followed up with Treehorn's Treasure.

REVOLTING BRIDESMAIDS
Mary Hooper
Puffin pbk £3.25
ISBN 0140368701

Katie is disgusted at all the fuss over her sister's impending marriage and what's worse, she has to be a bridesmaid in a fluffy blue dress. A great tomboy story which pokes fun at adult values.

HERE COMES CHARLIE MOON
Shirley Hughes
Red Fox pbk £2.50
ISBN 0099922304

Charlie and his cousin Ariadne are playing at their auntie's seaside shop and find themselves very busy. A breezy seaside romp of sideshows, mystery and mayhem.

THE HOUSE THAT SAILED AWAY
Pat Hutchins
Red Fox pbk £2.99
ISBN 0099932008

Something strange happens when Grandma comes to stay – the house sails away, down the street and off to sea, and, before long, the family encounters cannibals, pirates, a kidnapping and buried treasure in this slapstick adventure.

FOLLOW THAT BUS!
Pat Hutchins
Red Fox pbk £2.99
ISBN 0099932202

Class 6 should be going on an ordinary school trip until its absent-minded teacher switches her bag. The story becomes a fast-paced cops and robbers chase, making it a trip they will never forget!

VLAD THE DRAC
Ann Jungman
Collins pbk £2.99
ISBN 0006732720

Paul and Judy don't realise what they have let themselves in for when they take home a vampire as a holiday souvenir.

BLESSU & DUMPLING
Dick King-Smith
Puffin pbk £3.25
ISBN 0140346988

Blessu is an elephant with a problem – he gets hayfever! Sneezing so much makes his trunk stretch and stretch in this gentle story.

SOPHIE SERIES
Dick King-Smith
Walker pbk £3.50

Sophie is a wonderful creation from a master storyteller. She is witty, resourceful and imaginative as she gathers experience with animals to realise her dream of becoming a lady farmer. Begin the series with 'Sophie's Snail'.

SCARE YOURSELF TO SLEEP
Rose Impey
Collins pbk £3.99
ISBN 000674852X

Two cousins, staying in a tent at the bottom of the garden, try to scare each other with stories of invisible men and dustbin demons, but it works just a little too well. Great for reading beneath the bedclothes!

Did you know?

Many of Pat Hutchins' books have been influenced by her two sons. Titch was written for her elder son Morgan, and Sam, complaining of not having his own book, had 'Happy Birthday Sam' written for him. 'The House that Sailed Away' stars their whole family including Grandma and their cat!!

NAUGHTY STORIES
Barbara Ireson
Red Fox pbk £2.50
ISBN 0099699206

A funny, enjoyable and easy-to-read collection of stories, containing a host of mischievous characters. Authors include Dick King-Smith and Sheila Lavelle.

FIRST YOUNG PUFFIN BOOK OF BEDTIME STORIES
Barbara Ireson
Puffin pbk £3.99
ISBN 0140368094

Twenty-five ten minute stories about animals, school, dragons and much more. Authors include Joan Aiken, Philippa Pearce and Hazel Townson.

Follow That Bus

MY BEST FIEND
Sheila Lavelle
Puffin pbk £3.50
ISBN 0140371826

The first in the popular
'fiend' series. The 'fiend'
is Angela, Charlie's best
friend. Angela gets long-
suffering Charlie into all
sorts of scrapes and mishaps.
This funny book is a
collection of dreadful
deeds by two 'sweet' girls.

I DON'T WANT TO
Bel Mooney
Mammoth pbk £2.99
ISBN 0749704209

'I don't want to clean my
teeth', 'I don't want to eat
my vegetables'. There are
lots of things Kitty doesn't
want to do but being stubborn
leads to problems, and in
the end Kitty finds that saying
'yes', rather than 'no', isn't
so bad after all.

THE DANCING BEAR
Michael Morpurgo
Collins pbk £2.99
ISBN 0006745113

In a small mountain
village, orphaned Roxanne
finds an abandoned bear
cub, and soon they are
inseparable. The day comes
however, when Roxanne
must leave the village and
her bear. A deeply
moving story told with
great charm.

THE WORST WITCH
Jill Murphy
Puffin pbk £3.50
ISBN 0140311084

Mildred Hubble is a trainee
witch at Miss Cackle's
Academy for Witches and is
the worst pupil in the whole
school! The first in a hugely
popular series about school
life with a difference.

The Worst Witch

THE ENCHANTED HORSE
Magdalen Nabb
Collins pbk £2.99
ISBN 0006747213

Lonely and unhappy Irina is not looking forward to Christmas. Then she sees a shabby wooden horse in a junk shop and chooses it for her Christmas present, with magical consequences.

JOSIE SMITH
Magdalen Nabb
Collins pbk £2.99
ISBN 0006737447

The first book about Josie, her adventures and her understanding mother. These stories capture the child's world perfectly and gently unravel confusing childhood problems.

STONE MOUSE
Jenny Nimmo
Walker pbk £2.99
ISBN 0744531861

An enchanting story about a 'stone mouse', or a 'dirty old pebble' depending on whether you are a little girl called Elly, or her cross elder brother Ted.

THE LION AT SCHOOL
Philippa Pearce
Puffin pbk £3.50
ISBN 0140318550

Although 'India rubbers' and 'larders' will have to be translated for today's children, the quirky humour and strong narratives of these stories still appeal.

MRS PEPPERPOT STORIES
Alf Proysen
Red Fox pbk £3.99
ISBN 0099141213

Endearing tales of an old woman who shrinks to the size of a pepperpot at the most inconvenient moments. Plenty of humour and wit have kept these books popular for nearly 30 years.

Happy Families

Happy Families have been acclaimed as "the best thing to happen to beginner readers since Dr Seuss!" (Children's Right's Workshop). 'Mrs Vole and Vet' and 'Ms Cliffe the Climber' will be published in September. See Pg.33

My Best Fiend

THE DAY THE SMELLS WENT WRONG
Catherine Sefton
Puffin pbk £2.99
ISBN 0140370714

One day Jackie and Phil wake up to find that everything has changed its smell and the Chief Inspector of Smells needs help fast. A good story for children just starting to read on their own.

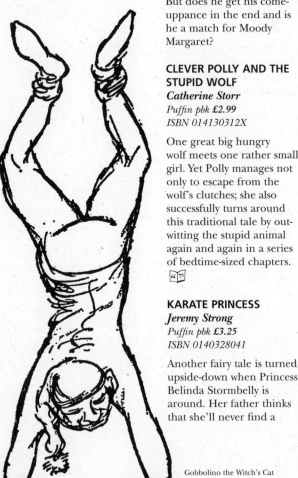

HORRID HENRY AND OTHER STORIES
Francesca Simon
Orion pbk £2.99
ISBN 1858810701

Henry is every teacher's troublemaker and every parent's nightmare. Henry is utterly horrid. He shouts and screams and stomps his way through four separate and easy to manage stories. But does he get his come-uppance in the end and is he a match for Moody Margaret?

CLEVER POLLY AND THE STUPID WOLF
Catherine Storr
Puffin pbk £2.99
ISBN 014130312X

One great big hungry wolf meets one rather small girl. Yet Polly manages not only to escape from the wolf's clutches; she also successfully turns around this traditional tale by out-witting the stupid animal again and again in a series of bedtime-sized chapters.

KARATE PRINCESS
Jeremy Strong
Puffin pbk £3.25
ISBN 0140328041

Another fairy tale is turned upside-down when Princess Belinda Stormbelly is around. Her father thinks that she'll never find a husband. However Belinda is an extraordinary young lady with some very funny ideas of her own!

THE OWL WHO WAS AFRAID OF THE DARK
Jill Tomlinson
Mammoth pbk £2.99
ISBN 074970795X

Plop, the baby barn owl, is afraid of the dark, but everyone he meets has reasons for liking the night and gradually Plop realises that the dark isn't so bad after all. This wonderful, reassuring book has been hailed as a modern classic.

GOBBOLINO THE WITCH'S CAT
Ursula Moray Williams
Puffin pbk £3.99
ISBN 0140302395

Born a witch's cat, Gobbolino doesn't want to be one. The story follows his search for a new home and a happy ending.

Gobbolino the Witch's Cat

Did you know?

Before he became a writer, Jeremy Strong worked picking strawberries, teaching and putting the jam in doughnuts. He has several pets, including a cat with a liking for olives, courgettes and pasta!

Fairy Tales

Fairy Tales and Mythology

Fairy Tales has become a generic term for what is, in fact, the oral heritage of Europe. They are the tales of ordinary people and of their imaginations. Too often dismissed as just stories for children, they are an invaluable way of looking at traditions of morality, humour and heroism in our history.

Most of the myths and legends in this section will be enjoyed by older children. The stories are complex and are more about power struggles and epic heroism and less about princesses and dragons. The non-European stories have exotic characters and locations but the themes are remarkably similar to more familiar tales.

Characters from Fairy Tales and Mythology will stay with children all their lives. Cinderella, Robin Hood and of course the dashing Prince will turn up in other guises again and again in literature. We have selected some of the best classic editions of these tales and also some more modern retellings. Take your pick.

Previous page: The Orchard
Book of Creation Stories Pg.48

Fairy Tales

Aesop

Aesop's fables have been around since the time of the Ancient Greeks. They are the original morality tales often with animals as the protagonists and often are a celebration of modesty over vanity. 'Actions Speak Louder Than Words', 'Look Before you Leap' and 'The Boy who Cried Wolf' are all the legacy of Aesop.

AESOP'S FABLES
Translated by S A Handford
Puffin pbk £3.99
ISBN 0140369848

AESOP'S FABLES
Translated by Sir Roger L'Estrange
Everyman hbk £7.99
ISBN 1857159004

CLASSIC FAIRY TALES
Puffin pbk £3.50-£4.50

Extensive versions of English, Irish, Scottish and Welsh Folk and Fairy Tales. These are attractive and affordable and a great introduction to the oral heritage of the British Isles, especially for teachers and parents.

The Brothers Grimm

The Grimm brothers began their record of oral literature early last century in Germany. They have immortalised such classic tales as 'Hansel and Gretel', 'Snow White' and 'Rumpelstiltskin' which are still read and enjoyed by children today.

GRIMM'S FAIRY TALES
Jacob and Wilhelm Grimm
Puffin pbk £3.50
ISBN 0140366962

FAIRY TALES
The Brothers Grimm, illustrations Arthur Rackham
Everyman hbk £9.99
ISBN 1857159055

Hans Christian Andersen

Danish Hans Andersen was a shoemaker's son and is credited with inventing the concept of Fairy Tales especially for children. His stories have all the dramatic elements of love, tragedy and the pursuit of happiness and yet are light and charming enough to hold a strong appeal for children.

FAIRY TALES
Hans Christian Andersen, illustrations Lisbeth Zwerger
Ragged Bears hbk £14.95
ISBN 0887081827

An outstanding gift edition of classic Andersen tales, illustrated in gentle, evocative watercolours to match the delicate prose.

STORIES FROM HANS ANDERSEN
Andrew Matthews, illustrations Alan Snow
Orchard hbk £9.99
ISBN 185213450X

All the favourites - Thumbelina, the Little Match Girl, the Ugly Duckling and others – appear in this collection. Alan Snow's witty and individual illustrations add humour and perfectly complement the lively, accessible text.

Oscar Wilde

Wilde said his stories were 'not for children but for childlike people' and and indeed they are subtle and melancholy in a very adult way. He drew much inspiration from Hans Andersen.

Orchard Book of Greek Myths

STORIES FOR CHILDREN
Oscar Wilde, illustrations PJ Lynch
Macdonald pbk £7.99
ISBN 0750009993

A lavish and stunningly illustrated collection of six of Wilde's best-loved fairy tales, including The Selfish Giant and The Happy Prince.

Modern Fairy Tales

The last twenty years have seen the traditional Fairy Tales turned upside down. Helpless princesses, wicked stepmothers, and triumphant wolves have all been overturned in preference for some more positive role models and less predictable outcomes.

FAIRY TALES
Terry Jones, illustrations Michael Foreman
Puffin pbk £3.99
ISBN 0140322620

Thirty new fairy tales full of fantasy from the ex-Monty Python member. Exciting and enthralling adventures with a host of magical characters make this a collection of modern classics, great for shared reading and ideal for reading aloud.

For more subversive and mixed-up Fairy Tales, look out for Jon Scieszka, Babette Cole (with the wonderful Princess Smartypants), Tony Ross and the Ahlbergs.

The best of the Anthologies

FIRST FAIRY TALES
Margaret Mayo, illustrations Selina Young
Orchard Books pbk £8.99
ISBN 1852135514

Nine favourite fairy tales re-told in rhyme and with repetition especially for young children. Ideal for reading aloud and great for shared reading, this collection is illustrated in bright, cheerful full-colour illustrations and contains classic tales such as Snow White and the Seven Dwarves, Hansel and Gretel and Cinderella.
4-6

THE WALKER BOOK OF FAIRY TALES
Amy Ehrlich, illustrations Diane Goode
Walker Books hbk £14.99
ISBN 0744503396

An enchanting collection of 19 classic fairy tales, beautifully illustrated and guaranteed to keep children spellbound. Stories include Elves and the Shoemaker, Rapunzel, Red Riding Hood, Jack and the Beanstalk, Hansel and Gretel and Rumpelstiltskin
5-8

ORCHARD BOOK OF FAIRY TALES
Rose Impey, illustrations Ian Beck
Orchard pbk £6.99
ISBN 1852138106

A collection of fourteen traditional fairy stories retold in a fresh and lively voice and illustrated in beautiful, soft watercolours. Tales include Puss in Boots, Cinderella, The Frog Prince and The Princess and the Pea.
5-8

Mythology and Folk Tales

THE PUFFIN CLASSICS MYTHS & LEGENDS
Roger Lancelyn Green
Puffin pbk £3.99 - 4.50

Amongst the Puffin Classics series are inspired retellings of myths and legends. Roger Lancelyn Green's concise prose makes sense of the vast complexity of the Greek Myths and the stories of the Trojan Wars and his enthusiasm invigorates the narrative. His tales of King Arthur are drawn from many sources, the most obvious being Malory, whose mood and poetry are echoed both in the language and the woodcuts which illustrate the text. These stories are full of excitement and drama. *Green's King Arthur is also available as an Everyman hbk.*

OXFORD MYTHS AND LEGENDS

WEST INDIAN FOLKTALES
Philip Sherlock
ISBN 0192741276 £4.99
SCOTTISH FOLK TALES AND LEGENDS
Barbara Ker Wilson
ISBN 0192741411 £4.99

The folktales and legends in this extensive series are retold with great vibrancy and freshness. Contemporary touches help capture the fun and strong presence of the storyteller in the tales of incorrigible Anansi the spider and Irraweka the mischief maker in West Indian folk-tales. In Scottish Folktales and Legends, the lovely melancholy of the seal wife is evoked and the heroic power of the deeds of Fionn MacChumail. The series also includes stories from India, China, Scandinavia and many other places.

THE ARABIAN NIGHTS
Brian Alderson &
Michael Foreman
Gollancz hbk £9.99
ISBN 0575058684

Brian Alderson brings the sheer magic of the Arabian Nights to life. Aladdin, Ali Baba and Sinbad all feature and each story is lavishly illustrated in wonderfully rich and exotic watercolours.

TALES OF ROBIN HOOD
Tony Allan
Usborne pbk £4.99
ISBN 0746020635

The exploits of the famous band of outlaws as they battle against the Sheriff of Nottingham are profusely illustrated in black and white and colour. The book has a final section which details the sources of the stories and even lists some of the many film versions.

BOOK OF MYTHOLOGY
Kingfisher hbk £14.99
ISBN 1856972364

This book provides a comprehensive look at world mythology, at gods, goddesses and heroes around the world. Fascinating introductions to different civilisations firmly place the myths in their contexts. The useful, easy to use index and glossary and rich illustration make this an invaluable reference work.

GREEK MYTHS FOR YOUNG CHILDREN
Marcia Williams
Walker pbk £4.99
ISBN 074453075X

Orpheus and Eurydice, Perseus and the Gorgon's Head and six other Greek myths retold in the style of a cartoon-strip for young children. The hilarious and detailed illustrations combine perfectly with an irreverent text to provide an entertaining introduction to these stories.

What is a myth?
A myth is more than just a good story. It is a story with a message. From the North American Plains to the Islands of Oceania, people have created a rich tapestry of spell-binding stories, characters and beliefs to explain the world around them.
Kingfisher Book of Mythology £14.99

ORCHARD BOOK OF GREEK MYTHS
Geraldine McCaughrean
Orchard hbk £10.99
ISBN 1852133732

This volume includes the famous adventures of Jason, Theseus and Odysseus and also less well-known tales such as the story of Arachne the spinner who boasted of her prowess and was turned into a spider by the gods. Lively text with appealing illustrations.

GREEK AND NORSE LEGENDS
Usborne pbk £7.99
ISBN 0746002408

An illustrated introduction to the world of Greek and Norse myths and legends. Simple plot outlines of the major stories combine with brief sketches of the main characters in an ideal reference work. The book includes a useful who's who of each mythology.

BLACK SHIPS BEFORE TROY
Rosemary Sutcliff, illustrations Alan Lee
Frances Lincoln hbk £12.99
ISBN 071120778X

Homer's epic poem 'The Iliad' is reworked with skill in Rosemary Sutcliff's version of the abduction of Helen by Paris of Troy and the ten-year war that ensued. The text is dramatically illustrated by renowned artist Alan Lee, whose haunting, detailed paintings bring Helen, Paris, Agamemnon, Achilles and all the other participants to life.
☆

ANANCY & MR DRYBONE
Fiona French
Frances Lincoln pbk £3.99
ISBN 0711207879

Prizewinning illustrator Fiona French creates an original story based on characters from traditional Caribbean and West African folktales. Both poor Anancy and rich Mr Dry-Bone want to marry the beautiful Miss Louise but she will only marry a man who can make her laugh. A superb interweaving of text and pictures.

SEASONS OF SPLENDOUR
Madhur Jaffrey
Puffin pbk £4.99
ISBN 0140346996

This is the best version of traditional tales from India available. Mainly based on the Hindu epics, it is beautifully illustrated by Michael Foreman.

STORY OF KING ARTHUR
Robin Lister
Kingfisher pbk £6.99
ISBN 086272970X

Robin Lister draws on a wide variety of sources as he unfolds the famous stories of King Arthur and his Round Table, of the doomed love of Lancelot and Guinevere, of the quest for the Holy Grail and Arthur's final defeat and departure for the magical Isle of Avalon. Alan Baker's evocative illustrations complement the text perfectly

BOOK OF CREATION STORIES
Margaret Mayo, illustrations Louise Brierley
Orchard hbk £12.99
ISBN 1852137746

A wonderful collection of stories from around the world which reveals the ways different cultures have explained how and why things began. Mayo's ten retellings are delightful to read alone, the text is clear enough for quite new readers, and even better to read aloud. Each story is complemented by illustrations which are soft and magical yet full of colour and vibrancy

The Orchard Book of Creation Stories

The Orchard Book of Creation Stories is part of a series of lavishly illustrated anthologies that includes Greek Myths, Nursery Rhymes, Magical Tales and Stories from the Ballet.

Page opposite: Alice in Wonderland

Fiction

Reading for 8-12 year olds

The mechanics of reading have been mastered by the time most children are eight and there is nothing to stop them from venturing into the wide world of independent reading. Everything is here from classics to contemporary prize winners, from easy-to-read comedy, to thought-provoking and complex novels, to magical and fantastic epics.

Some children will be itching to be let loose, others will look upon the vast choice with apprehension. You can find everything here that is in adult writing (humour, pathos, tragedy, science fiction, detective stories, romance) and children will become more discriminatory in their preferences for certain authors and genres, just as adults do.

To help choose the right book we have given a general age band with each title and of course there is the subject index at the back of the guide. Most of the authors featured have written several books and we are just offering a taste of some of their work. Scan the bookshelves for more of their titles.

Finn Family Moomintroll

WATERSHIP DOWN
Richard Adams
Puffin pbk £5.50
ISBN 014064536

This classic tale tells of the determination and courage of a group of rabbits fleeing from danger in search of a new home. Facing huge odds, Hazel leads them to a new life. Beautifully written, this story is touching,breath-taking and as a parable of 20th century living, very thought-provoking.
10–12

WOOF!
Allan Ahlberg
Puffin pbk £3.50
ISBN 0140319964

One night Eric is alarmed to find he has turned into a dog, and is even more puzzled to find he has changed back the next morning. Then it happens again at the swimming pool. Why does Eric keep changing and what can he do about it?
8–10

NECKLACE OF RAINDROPS
Joan Aiken
Puffin pbk £4.99
ISBN 0140307540

A magical collection of short stories which blend dream, fairy tales and myths into fantastic stories of a girl who lives in the sky, a giant cat, an airborne apple pie and other flights of the imagination. All stories are strikingly illustrated by Jan Pienkowski.
8–10

WOLVES OF WILLOUGHBY CHASE
Joan Aiken
Red Fox pbk £3.50
ISBN 0099972506

A nineteenth century that never was with James 3rd on the throne and wolves roaming the forests, provides the perfect background for this witty and dramatic tale peopled with marvellously Dickensian characters. Chief of these is the scheming Miss Slightcarp who has an evil plan. Blackhearts in Battersea is the compelling sequel.
10–12

THE HAUNTING OF CASSIE PALMER
Vivien Alcock
Mammoth pbk £3.50
ISBN 0749707089

Despite her mother's assurances that she will inherit psychic powers, Cassie doesn't believe in all that nonsense. Just to prove it, she tries to call up the spirit of a little girl, but raises the ambiguous Deveril from his grave instead.
10–12

LITTLE WOMEN
Louisa M Alcott
Puffin pbk £2.99
ISBN 0140366687

First published in 1868, Little Women remains compelling today. It is the story of the four March sisters, growing up in New England against the background of the American Civil War. Still both funny and moving, it also has wonderful Jo March – one of the ultimate, feisty heroines in children's books.
❝❞ 10–12

PAPER FACES
Rachel Anderson
Collins pbk £3.50
ISBN 0006746411

The moving story of a girl adapting to change and unfamiliar circumstances just after the second world war.
☆ 8–10

Necklace of Raindrops

THE TROUBLE WITH DONOVAN CROFT
Bernard Ashley
Puffin pbk £3.99
ISBN 0140309748

A poignant story about a family who foster an unhappy West Indian child, and the resulting disruption to family life. It deals sensitively with issues of racial prejudice.

10~12

THE INDIAN IN THE CUPBOARD
Lynne Reid Banks
Collins pbk £3.50
ISBN 0006730515

When Omri is given an old plastic Indian and an old bathroom cupboard for his birthday, it seems natural to keep them together. He has no idea that he will become responsible for the small but demanding and very real Indian.

 10~12

PETER PAN
JM Barrie
Puffin pbk £3.99
ISBN 0140320075

...or the boy who never grew up. Written originally as a play, this is the story of the three Darling children who fly with Peter to Never Never Land, with its Indians, Pirates and Tinkerbell the fairy. A book which never fails to enchant today with its mixture of magic and adventure.

10~12

THE WIZARD OF OZ
L Frank Baum
Puffin pbk £2.50
ISBN 0140350012

Every child knows the film and will find the book just as much fun. The story of Dorothy and her three friends, the Tin Woodman, the Scarecrow and the Cowardly Lion, and their magical journey along the yellow brick road is a delightful read.

10~12

CARRIE'S WAR
Nina Bawden
Puffin pbk £4.50
ISBN 0140364560

Carrie and her brother are evacuated to Wales during the Second World War, and find it hard to settle into their new home. They soon learn, however, to take advantage of their new-found freedom, which in turn liberates the people around them.

10~12

THE PEPPERMINT PIG
Nina Bawden
Puffin pbk £3.75
ISBN 0140309446

The feisty central character of Poll brings to life this story of a family's change

The Wizard of Oz

of circumstance at the turn of the century. Throughout a frequently difficult year, Johnnie, the Peppermint pig, the best thing about their new life, grows from a tiny piglet to fat maturity.

10~12

HACKER
Malorie Blackman
Transworld pbk £2.99
ISBN 0552527513

Vicky Gibb's father is accused of stealing over a million pounds from the bank where he works. Desperate to prove his innocence, Vicky learns about what really happened as well as about herself.

☆ 8~10

Judy Blume

Judy Blume's books are consistently warm, humorous and readable and have made her a much loved and respected author in many countries. She is best known for her ability to express the complex emotions children experience as they grow up, never shying away from difficult or embarrassing issues.

TALES OF A FOURTH GRADE NOTHING
Macmillan pbk £3.50
ISBN 0330262114

Nine year old Peter Hatcher's life is beset by problems. The biggest of which is his younger brother Fudge - and nobody appreciates quite what Peter has to go through! The first in several stories about Peter, Fudge and Sheila.

8~10

STARRING SALLY J FREEDMAN AS HERSELF
Macmillan pbk £3.50
ISBN 0330282794

It's 1947, and not even Sally's vivid imagination can comfort her when she has to move to Miami with her mother and brother, leaving her father behind - especially as she is convinced that the old man in her apartment block is really Adolf Hitler.

8~10

BLUBBER
Macmillan pbk £3.50
ISBN 0330263293

When the class begins to tease Linda about being fat, Jill Brenner is one of the ringleaders. However, when the tables are suddenly turned, she finds things aren't so funny on the other side.

10~12

IGGIE'S HOUSE
Macmillan pbk £3.50
ISBN 0330266829

Winnie's best friend Iggie has moved away and when a black family move into her old house Winnie becomes confused by the different reactions they cause in her white, middle class area. How should she respond to them? A thought-provoking read.

[📖] 10~12

ARE YOU THERE GOD? IT'S ME, MARGARET
Macmillan pbk £3.50
ISBN 0330262440

Growing up isn't easy, especially when no one really understands how you feel - so Margaret talks to God, hoping that somehow he will reveal to her the hundreds of things she wants to know.

[📖] 10~12

Enid Blyton

Probably one of the most well-known children's authors, and certainly the most prolific, Blyton's books have gone in and out of fashion with adults but have never lost their popularity with children. Her stories are formulaic, comfortable and escapist reads about adult-free worlds. Especially good for reluctant readers.

THE ENCHANTED WOOD
Mammoth pbk £3.50
ISBN 0749708034

Jo, Bessie and Fanny discover an enchanted wood, and the faraway tree at the top of which is a different land every time they visit. The first book in a series which follows the magical adventure they have with the fairy-folk of the woods.

[📖] 8~10

THE ISLAND OF ADVENTURE
Macmillan pbk £3.99
ISBN 0330333631

First in a series of stories in which four children and their talking parrot inadvertently fall into an adventure by way of the statutory secret passages and deserted mines. Guaranteed to capture the imagination of most children.

[📖] 8~10

David Henry Wilson

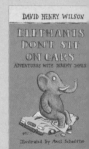

'Historic events surrounded my birth:
The King abdicated shortly before,
And then not long after, the whole planet Earth
Was rocked by a terrible war.

I don't think I caused that remarkable double –
I wasn't a soldier or a prince –
But I just didn't want to see any more trouble,
So I've been a good boy ever since.

Well, actually David Henry Wilson has probably been too busy to be bad. He teaches at two universities, translates books, participates in sport, writes and produces plays, and of course, writes wonderful children's books! Jeremy James is probably his best known character.

Some books by David Henry Wilson
Beside the Sea with Jeremy Jame
Getting Rich with Jeremy James
Do Goldfish Play the Violir
Please Keep off the Dinosau
Do Gerbils Go to Heaven
Elephants Don't Sit on Cars
(all published by Macmillan)

THE CHILDREN OF GREEN KNOWE
Lucy M Boston
Puffin pbk £3.99
ISBN 0140364617

When Tolly goes to live with his great-grandmother, little does he know what a wonderful time he will have, for hers is a very special house which Tolly finds he is sharing with children who lived many years ago.

8–10

THE SCHOOL AT THE CHALET
Elinor Brent-Dyer
Collins pbk £3.50
ISBN 0006925170

A young English woman decides to set up a school for girls in the Austrian Tyrol - a cosmopolitan environment in which many adventures take place. First published in 1926, this is the first in a long and much- loved series about the Chalet school.

10–12

WHISPERS IN THE GRAVEYARD
Theresa Breslin
Mammoth pbk £3.50
ISBN 0749723882

Solomon, a dyslexic, let down by his parents and his teachers, suddenly finds himself called upon to save a young girl from a dreadful fate. A gripping novel, which sets stark social realism against a tense psychological and supernatural drama.

☆ 10–12

The Man

THE MAN
Raymond Briggs
Red Fox pbk £5.99
ISBN 009910881X

When John finds The Man in his room one night, a strange, complicated and extraordinary friendship begins. Exploring a wealth of emotions from anger and curiosity to selfishness and jealousy, it is an unsentimental examination of relationships with wonderful illustrations.

8–10

RUDLEY CABOT IN THE CARROTS OF DOOM
Keith Brumpton
Orion pbk £3.99
ISBN 1858811538

The comic strip adventures of Rudley Cabot, rabbit extraordaire, are ideal for children immersed in TV culture. There is some text but mainly speech bubbles and it is divided into 'episodes' rather than chapters. 'Carrots of Doom' is the second 'fur-raising' title available featuring pyramids, ancient scrolls, and the foiling of a kidnap attempt using Iceberg lettuces...

8–10

A LITTLE PRINCESS
Frances Hodgson Burnett
Puffin pbk £3.50
ISBN 0140366881

Privileged Sarah Crewe, star pupil at Miss Minchin's Academy, is reduced to servant status when her father loses his fortune - but, nevertheless, she retains her dignity, good spirits and several close friends. A fairy-tale like story, loved by generations of children, in which purity and courage triumph over corruption.

10–12

THE SECRET GARDEN
Frances Hodgson Burnett
Puffin pbk £2.50
ISBN 0140366660

After the death of her parents, contrary Mary Lennox is brought from India to live in her uncle's enormous house in Yorkshire. Here she discovers a 'secret garden' and slowly learns to enjoy the world around her. A beautifully-written story which explores the emotional development of several characters.

10–12

THE INCREDIBLE JOURNEY
Sheila Burnford
Hodder pbk £3.99
ISBN 0340626658

Follow the adventures of a labrador, a bull terrier and a Siamese cat as they travel through the wilderness to find their home. A classic story of courage and loyalty for all animal lovers, upon which the Disney film 'Homeward Bound' was based.

10–12

CASTLE OF FEAR
Patrick Burston
Walker pbk £4.99
ISBN 0744517419

Part of an excellent series of large format adventure game books for younger children. There are mazes, puzzles and objects to find on each absorbing page, as well as the all-important choice of which page to turn to next to complete the mission.

8–10

COMPUTER NUT
Betsy Byars
Red Fox pbk £2.99
ISBN 0099425912

When Kate starts getting messages on her computer from an 'alien' she is sure someone is playing a joke on her, until the messages become more and more convincing...A fun read from an author well known for her perception of children's thoughts and feelings.

8–10

THE EIGHTEENTH EMERGENCY
Betsy Byars
Puffin pbk £3.25
ISBN 0140308636

Benjie Fawley - known as Mouse to his friends - has an emergency plan for all possible dangers. But when Big Man Hammerman decides to get him he finds that perhaps he is not such a mouse after all.

8–10

ALICE IN WONDERLAND
Lewis Carroll
Puffin pbk £3.50
ISBN 0140301690

A brilliant, funny and frequently surreal child's-eye view of a nonsensical, illogical world. Alice's Adventures in Wonderland and Through the Looking Glass are undisputed classics, having given us some of the best known and best-loved characters in children's literature. Through the Looking Glass is also available from Puffin and several gift versions are in print. Look out for the lovely Macmillan editions with Tenniel's illustrations.
8–10

SOCCER AT SANDFORD
Rob Childs
Transworld pbk £2.99
ISBN 044086318X

A book for the football-mad reluctant reader, which follows the excitements and disappointments of the talented young footballers at Sandford Primary School during one season.
8–10

TRIPODS TRILOGY
John Christopher
Puffin pbk £5.99
ISBN 0140317228

When Will Parker runs away from home to escape the ritual 'Capping' ceremony, he begins a life of adventure and danger as a member of the human rebellion against the Earth's alien masters and their fearsome fighting machines, the Tripods.
10–12

RAMONA QUIMBY AGED 8
Beverly Cleary
Puffin pkk £3.75
ISBN 0140315608

Meet Ramona Quimby, the ebullient young girl whose plans always seem to go wrong – with hilarious results! Children will relish Ramona's crazy adventures.

UNDER THE HAWTHORN TREE
Marita Conlon-McKenna
Puffin pbk £3.50
ISBN 014036031X

The Irish famine of the 1840s is dramatically brought to life in this epic tale. Three brave children undertake the treacherous journey to Castle Taggart to find their fabled great-aunts. A heart-rending tale of courage and strength.
(Irish edition by O'Brien Press ISBN 0862782066)
10–12

WHAT KATY DID
Susan Coolidge
Puffin pbk £2.99
ISBN 0140366970

Written at about the same time as Little Women, and also American, this is a very different book. The story of irrepressible Katy Carr who always means to be good as an angel but never quite manages it!
10–12

THE DARK IS RISING SEQUENCE
Susan Cooper
Puffin pbk £9.99
ISBN 0140316884

Omnibus edition of the thrilling fantasy series, which is rich in myth and Celtic legend and bristling with atmosphere. Individual titles also available.
10–12

BULLY
Yvonne Coppard
Red Fox pbk £2.99
ISBN 0099838605

When Kerry starts at a new school following a crash that has left her permanently disabled, she is mercilessly teased and tormented. A realistic and very readable story about the problems of bullying and about the emotional aftermath of a serious accident.
10–12

THE STEPS UP THE CHIMNEY
William Corlett
Red Fox pbk £2.99
ISBN 0099853701

Three children spend the Christmas holidays at their uncle's creepy old house in the remote Welsh borders and discover its magic secrets. This is the first nail-biting book in The Magician's House quartet.
10–12

MY TEACHER IS AN ALIEN
Bruce Coville
Collins pbk £2.99
ISBN 0006940811

Susan Simmons just knows there is something weird about her new teacher, but when she finds out he is an alien who can she trust to believe her?

10-12

MOONDIAL
Helen Cresswell
Puffin pbk £3.99
ISBN 0140325239

When Minty goes to stay with her aunt she becomes fascinated by the big house across the road. She discovers a mysterious moondial in the garden, which opens a door to the past, where two unhappy children need her help.

10-12

THE DEMON HEADMASTER
Gillian Cross
Puffin pbk £3.50
ISBN 0140316434

From the first day, Dinah can tell that her new school isn't normal. Immaculate, regimented children recite facts and dates in the playground, and there's a whiff of fear in the air. What, or who, are they frightened of?

10-12

THE GREAT ELEPHANT CHASE
Gillian Cross
Puffin pbk £3.99

ISBN 0140363610

Two children travel across America, drawing on their instinct for survival and the power of their friendship, as they struggle to save their elephant from exploitation. An exhilarating adventure.

☆ 10-12

Roald Dahl

Roald Dahl is one of the most popular children's writers in print. His witty and, at times, disturbing prose addresses many issues that matter to children. His genius is the product of a sense of humour and an ability to understand what it is about stories that children like. His own experiences as a child, recounted in 'Boy' are to be found in his writing – being ignored or mistreated are recurrent themes. His humorous heroes and heroines always win battles against adult injustice and oppression. The books are funny and the plots fantastic; children know that Roald Dahl is on their side.

THE BFG
Puffin pbk £4.50
ISBN 0140315977

Sophie the orphan is kidnapped by a giant and fears she will be eaten. She has, however, been taken by a big friendly giant, and together they hatch a clever plan to stop the other giants eating children ever again.

8-10

The BFG

BOY & GOING SOLO
Puffin pbk £6.99
ISBN 0140349170

The autobiographies of Roald Dahl, which include both the fantastic and horrible things which happened to him, echoes of which can be found in his books. Funny, sad and fascinating.

10-12

CHARLIE & THE CHOCOLATE FACTORY
Puffin pbk £4.50
ISBN 0140371540

Poverty-stricken Charlie is amazed to find he has won a trip to Willy Wonka's amazing chocolate factory, along with four horrible children. As the fantastic tour goes on the others get distracted by the magical sweets until there is just Charlie left, and then he finds out exactly what wonderful prize he has won.

8-10

DANNY, CHAMPION OF THE WORLD
Puffin pbk £4.50
ISBN 0140371575

Danny and his father live together in a small caravan, each devoted to the other. Danny thinks he knows everything about his father until he discovers he's a secret poacher. He persuades his father to let him help and they plan the biggest poaching outing ever!

 8-10

JAMES AND THE GIANT PEACH
Puffin pbk £3.99
ISBN 0143042699

James lives with his awful aunts who make his life a misery. The growth of an amazing giant peach in their garden changes his life, as its inhabitants – some magical giant insects – rescue James and take him on a fantastic journey.

 8-10

MATILDA
Puffin pbk £4.50
ISBN 0140327592

A little girl escapes the loneliness of her world and the unpleasantness of her family through reading books. This opens her mind to psychic powers which she uses to save her beloved class teacher and schoolmates from their bullying headmistress. A thought-provoking book about the ill treatment of children, handled in a light- hearted way.

8-10

THE WITCHES
Puffin pbk £4.50
ISBN 0140317309

The witches of England hatch a plan to turn all the children into mice. They test the potion on the one boy who has been warned about these ghastly hags by his wise grandmother. He must then use his new mousy wits to survive and plan his revenge upon them. This book has a surprising ending, which, although unconventional, fits the story perfectly.

☆ 8-10

Don't forget all the other great titles …

CHARLIE & THE GREAT GLASS ELEVATOR

ESIO TROT

GEORGE'S MARVELLOUS MEDICINE

THE TWITS

SWAN SISTER
Annie Dalton
Mammoth pbk £2.99
ISBN 0749710659

Ellen is the only person to realise the danger her baby sister is in, but can she stop the terrible event from happening? This is an exceptional and moving story.

8-10

The Witches

KITTENS IN THE KITCHEN
Lucy Daniels
Hodder pbk £2.99
ISBN 034060722X

Mandy is an animal lover
and helps her parents in
their veterinary surgery.
When a stray cat has
unwanted kittens in a neighbour's kitchen, Mandy has
only a week to find homes
for the lot. The first book in
a popular animal series.

8–10

THE ANIMALS OF
FARTHING WOOD
Colin Dann
Mammoth pbk £3.99
ISBN 0749710667

When their forest home is
threatened by the bulldoz-
ers, the animals realise they
must look for a new home.
They set off on a perilous
journey to a nature reserve,
during which they must face
death, danger and disaster
before they are safe. An
unsentimental story which
portrays wild animal life and
its accompanying dangers.

📖 ☆ 10–12

EARTH TO MATTHEW
Paula Danziger
Macmillan pbk £2.99
ISBN 0330325019

Matthew Martin is always
clowning around, irritating
his sister and his classmates.
To be allowed to go on the
school trip he must start
behaving like a sensible
human being, and take
the class ecology project
seriously.

8–10

The Great Smile Robbery P.75

MAKE LIKE A TREE AND
LEAVE
Paula Danziger
Macmillan pbk £2.99
ISBN 0330322257

Matthew is out to annoy
everyone around him, but
when a favourite teacher has
an accident and her house is
to be sold to make way for a
shopping development,
Matthew and his friends
rally round to save the land.
Hilariously written and full
of slapstick comedy.

8–10

CONRAD'S WAR
Andrew Davies
Scholastic pbk £1.75
ISBN 0590700103

Conrad is obsessed by war,
so when he's transported
back to the Second World
War and trapped in Colditz
Castle, he knows what to do
– he's seen 'The Guns of
Navarone'. But what is his
Dad, the fat author, doing
there too?

10–12

EDUCATING MARMALADE
Andrew Davies
Puffin pbk £3.25
ISBN 0140370277

This side-splitting story follows the exploits of Marmalade, a girl with no intention of being brain-washed into being good.

8–10

FIRST TERM AT TREBIZON
Anne Digby
Puffin pbk £3.25
ISBN 0140324186

It is Rebecca Mason's first term at the famous Trebizon school and she longs to make an impression with a piece for the school magazine. What ensues is a scandal which rocks the whole school. First in a popular series.

10–12

STREET CHILD
Berlie Doherty
Collins pbk £3.50
ISBN 0006740200

The true story of Jim, an orphan who ran away from the workhouse in the 1860s, and whose plight inspired Doctor Barnardo to set up his children's homes.

10–12

THE HOUSE OF RATS
Stephen Elboz
Collins pbk £3.50
ISBN 0006748120

This is a mysterious tale of four children whose lives are thrown into turmoil when 'the master' of the house where they live leaves. Hitherto rigidly obeyed rules are broken and danger lurks.

☆ 10–12

MOONFLEET
JM Falkner
Puffin pbk £3.50
ISBN 0140367047

This classic tale of 18th Century smugglers has all the ingredients of a good yarn - buried treasure, dark deeds, the curse of Colonel 'Blackbeard' Mohune and some deliciously horrible encounters with corpses in dark tunnels.

10–12

CHARLOTTE SOMETIMES
Penelope Farmer
Puffin pbk £4.25
ISBN 0140360840

Off to boarding school for the first time, Charlotte discovers an unexpected problem; she has slipped back to 1918 with a different personality and the name Clare. Time-travel is confusing and tiring. Then Clare disappears – will Charlotte be stuck in 1918 for good?

10–12

Charlotte's Web Pg. 65

Anne Fine

Multi-award-winning Anne Fine writes with humour and understanding about difficult issues. Very well-written and very readable, her books have been adapted for television and the cinema.

FLOUR BABIES
Anne Fine
Puffin pbk £3.99
ISBN 0140361472

The flour babies are bags of flour which class 4C, much to their disgust, have to care for night and day for three weeks as part of the school science fair. Gradually, in this funny and tender story, the class become aware of the responsibilities of parenthood.
☆ 「💬」 10-12

GOGGLE EYES
Anne Fine
Puffin pbk £3.75
ISBN 0140340718

The humorous and touching account of how a girl learns to accept her mother's new boyfriend.
☆ 「💬」 10-12

MIDNIGHT BLUE
Pauline Fisk
Lion pbk £3.50
ISBN 0745919251

Bonnie has always known there was a land beyond the sky. In a balloon of midnight blue, she travels to this mirror world, where she learns to make sense of her relationship with her mother

and to challenge the sinister power of Grandbag. Emotionally complex, and beautifully written.
☆ 10-12

HARRIET THE SPY
Louise Fitzhugh
Collins pbk £3.50
ISBN 0006721753

Sparky Harriet wants to be a spy. Her training involves following, and making notes on everyone in her neighbourhood, including her friends. Her comments are honest, rather than flattering, so she is less than popular when her notebook is discovered!
10-12

WAR BOY
Michael Foreman
Puffin pbk £3.50
ISBN 0140342990

Foreman writes and illustrates his own war-time childhood memories of a Suffolk village, where his mother owned a corner shop. An informative, humorous and moving account of the war. A gift edition is also available *(Pavilion, ISBN 1851453539)*
8-10

MONKEY ISLAND
Paula Fox
Orchard pbk £3.99
ISBN 185213853X

Abandoned by his mother, Clay finds himself living rough in New York. This enthralling, but unglamor-

ised tale deals with issues of family, homelessness and fostering.
10-12

THE WEIRDSTONE OF BRISINGAMEN
Alan Garner
Collins pbk £3.99
ISBN 0006742939

Colin and Susan meet a wizard and creatures from the underworld, as their own lives get mixed up with the magic of ancient legends.
10-12

THE FAMILY FROM ONE END STREET
Eve Garnett
Puffin pbk £3.99
ISBN 0140367756

Winner of the Carnegie Medal, this book was first published in 1937 and was intended to highlight the poverty of urban children between the wars. However, it quickly established itself as an entertaining story of family life and remains timelessly enjoyable.
☆ 8-10

Ruth Thomas

Ruth was a teacher in London, Southend and Plymouth before she retired early to take up travelling. Somehow she started writing instead!
The Runaways, her first book, won the Guardian Children's Fiction Prize in 1987 and she has written several books since then.

'Punchy, compassionate, good-humoured ... children will love it'
The Independent on 'The Class that Went Wild'

'Ruth Thomas's portrayal of the subtleties of primary school relationships ... and her ear for the cadences and idiosyncratic logic of their talk combine with a fierce emotional suspense to make a riveting read for kids and an eye-opener for adults'
The Bookseller

Books by Ruth Thomas

The Runaways
Guilty
The Hideaway
The New Boy
The Class that Went Wild
The Secret
(All published by Hutchinson & Red Fox)

'If anyone is more on the wavelength of 9-11 year olds I would like to know'
The Observer

Morris Gleitzman

Born in England but now living in Australia, Morris Gleitzman has written many excellent and compelling children's books. His stories tend to be very funny and rather off-beat, despite dealing with some serious issues, such as illness, death and disability.

Asterix

BLABBER MOUTH
Macmillan pbk £3.50
ISBN 033033283X

A moving, yet funny story about a mute girl starting at a new school and trying to be accepted, despite her differences. Being constantly embarrassed by her outrageous father doesn't help!

10-12

TWO WEEKS WITH THE QUEEN
Macmillan pbk £3.50
ISBN 0330313762

Luke has cancer, and his brother Colin decides that the one person who could help is the Queen. Crazy attempts to contact her ensue, including phone calls to the Royale Fish Bar, Peckham. Complex issues approached with humour and directness.

10-12

ASTERIX SERIES
Goscinny & Uderzo
Hodder pbk £4.99

Nowhere else can you shudder at more excruciating puns, engage in more utterly gratuitous (and equally harmless) violence, and at the same time learn rather a lot of bona fide Roman History. Wordplay, running jokes and ironic cultural stereotyping, make for witty texts and storylines. The accomplished, satirical cartoon style of the pictures is unfailingly inventive.

Asterix and his Gaulish compatriots get their indomitable strength from Getafix's magic potion, and with great humour, portray much about human frailty.

8-10

Did you Know?

• Illustrator Uderzo is colour blind

• that Sean Connery and the Beatles make guest appearances in the books

• that even to this day no one really knows exactly what goes into the Magic Potion

Find out more in The Complete Guide to Asterix by Peter Kessler

---

ASTERIX GAME BOOKS
Hodder pbk £5.99

These game books are based on the cartoon books and have an extra, interactive dimension to them (Famous Five and others also available). The child uses the dice, map and other effects to crack codes, solve mysteries and determine the course of the plot. Perfect for reluctant readers as they introduce characters which can then be followed up later in the more 'conventional' format novels.

8-10

THE DIDDAKOI
Rumer Godden
Macmillan pbk £3.50
ISBN 0330323970

Kizzy doesn't care that she's teased at school for being half gypsy – a 'diddakoi'. She lives in a caravan with her Gran and Old Joe the caravan horse, and everything is fine – until her Gran dies, and the world she knows and loves comes under threat.

10–12

LITTLE WHITE HORSE
Elizabeth Goudge
Lion pbk £3.50
ISBN 0745914586

A delightful, engaging fairy tale about the sun Merryweathers and the moon Merryweathers, and their tendency to quarrel. Maria is determined to stop the quarrels for good and end the disharmony that mars the otherwise idyllic Moonacre valley.

☆ 8–10

THE WIND IN THE WILLOWS
Kenneth Grahame
Puffin pbk £2.99
ISBN 0140366857

The immortal story of Mole, Ratty, Badger and Toad and their lives along the banks of the river, messing about in boats or attempting to defeat the weasels and stoats in the Wild Wood. Very much a book of its time, but one that retains pertinence through its vivid and humorous characterisation.

📖 8–10

THE WIZARD OF EARTHSEA
Ursula le Guin
Puffin pbk £3.99
ISBN 0140364609

After Sparrowhawk uses magic to save his village, he is sent to the school for Wizards to learn to control his power. There his boastful pride betrays him and he unwittingly releases a dark force in the world that pursues him to the ends of the earth. First in a series.

10–12

THE LAST VAMPIRE
Willis Hall
Red Fox pbk £2.99
ISBN 0099115417

Henry Hollins and his parents are on their first trip abroad, travelling around Europe. They end up at the castle Alucard which appears to be deserted - but is it? The villagers are acting very strangely too - what's going on? A hilarious tale with more in the series to enjoy as well.

📖 8–10

WHERE'S WALLY
Martin Handford
Walker pbk £4.99
ISBN 0744510996

What started as a simple, ingenious idea, has become an international phenomenon, and children all over the world know how to find Wally, Wenda and the others in the closely populated pictures. Enjoy the visual jokes and intricate detail in these compulsive and increasingly complex books.

8–10

THE WOOL PACK
Cynthia Harnett
Puffin pbk £4.50
ISBN 0140301534

An historical novel set at the end of the 15th Century. The action takes place in Winchester and the Cotswolds and is full of adventure and suspense.

10–12

The Wind in the Willows

WITCHES
Colin and Jacqui Hawkins
Collins pbk £3.50
ISBN 0001981668

Previously available as a picture book, and now in standard novel format. Children will love the wacky illustrations, daft jokes and basic witch information like wardrobe essentials, diet, hobbies etc. 'Vampires', 'Spooks', 'Pirates' and others also available.

 8–10

LISTEN TO THE DARK
Maeve Henry
Mammoth pbk £2.99
ISBN 074971784X

The discovery of a long-buried family secret has a profound effect on Mark, an awkward adolescent boy, and on his relationship with his possessive mother and uncommunicative father. An uncompromising, but ultimately optimistic book.

☆ 10–12

Ten thousand thundering typhoons!... Now I'm going to chuck you out of the window!

Tintin

THE ADVENTURES OF TINTIN
Hergé
Mammoth pbk £3.99

Hergé combines his precise, easy and immediately recognisable visual style with good-natured, adventure-packed stories in over 20 different books. From the wry linguistic humour of 'The Broken Ear' to the hard-nosed industrial espionage of 'The Calculus Affair' and the heart-warming pathos of 'Tintin in Tibet'. With a cast of wonderfully rounded and instantly recognisable characters, there are adventures for all sorts of moods and all sorts of readers.

8–10

SEE YA SIMON
David Hill
Puffin pbk £3.50
ISBN 0140363815

Simon's body is being wasted by muscular dystrophy, but his spirit does not falter. He lives with wit, insight and determination. Seen through the eyes of his best friend Nathan, the last year of Simon's life is not the last year of friendship.

10–12

BEAVER TOWERS
Nigel Hinton
Puffin pbk £3.25
ISBN 0140370609

Philip is flown by magic to an island where the beavers, Mr Edgar and Baby B, and their friends are the last resistance against the evil witch, Oyin. It seems that Philip is to be their unlikely saviour!

8–10

THE MOUSE AND HIS CHILD
Russell Hoban
Puffin pbk £3.99
ISBN 0140308415

When the clockwork mouse and his child break, they are thrown away, and so begins a quest for self winding, for a home and a return to the happiness they once knew in the toyshop. Adventure and much more abounds.

8–10

I AM DAVID
Anne Holm
Mammoth pbk £3.99
ISBN 0749701366

When David escapes from prison camp and 'them', he faces a long and difficult journey, the unlearning of fear, and the learning of hope.

10–12

GROOSHAM GRANGE
Anthony Horowitz
Walker pbk £3.99
ISBN 0744547121

What kind of school collects its new pupils in a hearse, and makes them sign in blood? Packed full of quick fire jokes that make you laugh and groan and a cast of weird characters straight out of a spoof horror film.

10–12

THE·IRON MAN
Ted Hughes
Faber pbk £3.99
ISBN 0571141498

The huge Iron Man roams the land, and feeds on old cars and machinery. Hailed as a modern classic, this tale contains some startling imagery, which makes it a rich and rewarding book.

10~12

THE IRON WOMAN
Ted Hughes
Faber pbk £3.99
ISBN 057117163X

The Iron Woman rises silently screaming from the mire to exact punishment on mankind for polluting the earth. It is their last chance to make amends, and while the women and children watch and wait, every man in Britain experiences the horror of pollution at first hand (or first fin, as it turns out).

8~10

The Iron Woman

THE SECRET OF PLATFORM 13
Eva Ibbotson
Macmillan pbk £3.50
ISBN 0330337483

Under platform 13 at King's Cross Station, there is a gump. It is open for 9 days, every 9 years and the last time it was open, a royal prince was stolen. Now a hand-picked team must rescue him, even though he's not very cooperative.

10~12

WHICH WITCH
Eva Ibbotson
Macmillan pbk £2.99
ISBN 0330265865

Arriman the Awful is looking for a wife - the blackest witch of a wife he can find in Todcaster. Belladonna would so like it to be her - the trouble is, she is irredeemably white.

8~10

THE WARLOCK OF FIRETOP MOUNTAIN
Steve Jackson and Ian Livingstone
Puffin pbk £3.99
ISBN 0140315381

First of a hugely popular fantasy series of adventure game books. The player has a quest and by making certain choices along the way, fighting many battles and using a lot of skill it is possible to reach the ultimate goal. If not, start again and take a different route.

10~12

Finn Family Moomintroll

Robin Jarvis

The thoroughly gripping, fast-paced books of Robin Jarvis contain themes of good versus evil. They involve sorcery, mystery, terror and are full of strange beasts, witches and even a foul-mouthed teddy bear who talks with an American drawl. The human, animal and magical worlds entwine in the three series he has written and 'The Woven Patch' marks the beginning of his fourth.

DEPTFORD HISTORIES
ALCHEMIST'S CAT
OAKEN THRONE
THOMAS

DEPTFORD MICE
DARK PORTAL
CRYSTAL PRISON
FINAL RECKONING

WHITBY SERIES
WHITBY WITCHES
THE WHITBY CHILD
All Macdonald Young Books
£4.99

WYRD MUSEUM
THE WOVEN PATH
Collins pbk £4.99
0006750125

10-12

Did you know?

Did you know that Robin Jarvis , bestselling author of the Whitby and Deptford trilogies was born three weeks late on a sofa in Liverpool!

REDWALL SERIES
Brian Jacques
Red Fox pbk £4.50 each

The Redwall books have become one of the best-selling series of the last 10 years. The first one, 'Redwall' was nominated for the Carnegie award and with eight currently in the series there is plenty to keep even the most avid reader going! Populated with warrior otters, brave mousemaids and cut-throat weasels, this is an exciting and unmiss-able series.

10-12

FINN FAMILY MOOMINTROLL
Tove Jansson
Puffin pbk £3.99
ISBN 014030150X

When Moomintroll finds a tall, black hat, he has no idea that it belongs to a hobgoblin - but everyone notices when peculiar things begin to happen. These magical stories about the Moomins (small, fat, endearing beasts), manage to combine strange, almost surreal elements with comfortingly familiar domestic detail.

8-10

UNREAL!
Paul Jennings
Puffin pbk £3.50
ISBN 0140370994

A collection of character-istically quirky stories from a master of the bizarre. Bones that want to be reunited, ghosts that play 'we shall not be moved' on the clarinet and saxophone - these strange tales will delight children with active imaginations.

10-12

Brian Jacques

Brian Jacques has been a lorry driver, a stand-up comedian, a docker and a playwright! However, most children know him as the author of the epic and bestselling Redwall Abbey books.

Brian Jacques loves gangster films, dogs, chilli con carne, dry red wine, and kids. He hates football, sit-coms, hot milk, phoney accents, woolly pullovers and windy days!

'Mr Jacques is a good storyteller ... he lifts the reader by the sheer panache of his writing'
Junior Bookshelf

The first book 'Redwall' was published in 1986 and was nominated for the Carnegie award. When he was writing it he used to carry it about in a shopping bag!

Currently numbering eight in the series, here are the Redwall books:

Redwall	**Martin the Warrior**
Mossflower	**The Bellmaker**
Mattimeo	**Outcast of Redwall**
Mariel of Redwall	*(All published by Red Fox)*
Salamandastron	

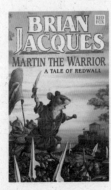

THE SAGA OF ERIK THE VIKING
Terry Jones
Puffin pbk £3.99
ISBN 0140322612

In a ship called the Golden Dragon, Erik and his brave band of men sail in search of 'the land where the sun goes at night'. Told with Jones' inimitable style and humour, each exciting chapter is a story in itself.

☆ 8–10

THE LIVES OF CHRISTOPHER CHANT
Diana Wynne Jones
Mammoth pbk £3.50
ISBN 0749700335

Evil forces, mysterious powers and strange worlds all combine to make this unusual and exciting tale. You just have to keep reading to discover if Christopher can defeat the enemies before his time is up.

10–12

THE PHANTOM TOLLBOOTH
Norman Juster
Collins pbk £3.99
ISBN 0006725880

Milo was bored, very bored - until he met a ticking watchdog called 'Tock', the smallest giant in the world, a mathamagician and many, many other puzzling characters. Milo has no time to be bored and nor will the reader if they pick up this intriguing book.

8–10

EMIL & THE DETECTIVES
Eric Kastner
Red Fox pbk £3.50
ISBN 0099293617

After being robbed, Emil is let down by unbelieving authorities. With a group of youngsters he turns private eye and seeks justice in this classic detective story.

 8–10

SECRET CLUES
Fiona Kelly
Hodder pbk £3.50
ISBN 0340588675

Secret Clues is the first book in the Mystery Club series. The three friends try to solve clues to a lost fortune and find themselves involved in a mysterious adventure. A good start to a gripping series of books.

10–12

THE TURBULENT TERM OF TYKE TILER
Gene Kemp
Puffin pbk £3.50
ISBN 0140311351

Tyke and Danny Price struggle through everyday problems in their last term of primary school. Hilarious and with a clever twist which is never quite revealed.

☆ 8–10

WHEN HITLER STOLE PINK RABBIT
Judith Kerr
Collins pbk £3.99
ISBN 0006708013

The first book in a trilogy based on the experiences of the author's own family during World War Two. Anna and her family escape from the Nazis, encountering more difficulties with each step of their journey.

10–12

STIG OF THE DUMP
Clive King
Puffin pbk £4.50
ISBN 0140364501

Stig of the Dump is full of secrets. How do you tell your Grandma that you are playing with a stone-age boy? How do you believe it yourself when you return a year later for another 'boring' holiday with Gran? Though fantastical, this book is really about the friendship of children in a sometimes dangerous world.

8–10

When Hitler stole Pink Rabbit

THE SHEEP PIG
Dick King-Smith
Puffin pbk £3.50
ISBN 0140318399

Dick King-Smith has the knack of turning mundane creatures into wonderful heroes. Who would believe a pig could talk ...but that would be telling. This is an exciting and touching story about an unlikely hero.

 8–10

THE QUEEN'S NOSE
Dick King-Smith
Puffin pbk £3.25
ISBN 0140318380

The combination of richly observed reality, from a child's point of view, and fantastical magic makes 'The Queen's Nose' enchanting. The reality starts in an old smelly chicken hut at the bottom of a wet suburban garden. The magic starts when this dull scene is transformed by our heroine's imagination into a pagoda in an Indian jungle.

8–10

THE JUNGLE BOOK
Rudyard Kipling
Puffin pbk £2.99
ISBN 0140366865

The well-known and well-loved story of Mowgli, the man-cub brought up by wolves and taught the law of the jungle. The book also contains other stories from India, including Rikki-tikki-tavi the Mongoose, and Toomai of the Elephants.

 8–10

JUST SO STORIES
Rudyard Kipling
Puffin pbk £2.99
ISBN 0140367020

From the elephant's child with his insatiable curiosity, to how the whale got his throat, these timeless stories have been enjoyed by generations of children.

 8–10

HIDING OUT
Elizabeth Laird
Mammoth pbk £3.50
ISBN 0149716649

What would you do if you were left behind with no food, no money, no home and nobody? Peter has to find the answers to these questions the hard way. A very credible and well written story.

☆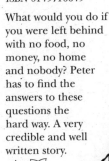
10–12

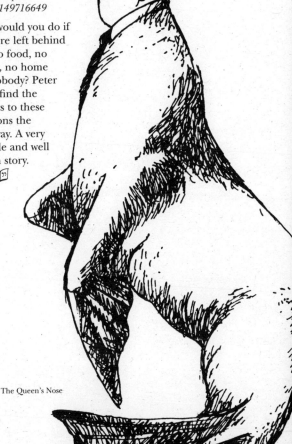

The Queen's Nose

THE FIB AND OTHER STORIES
George Layton
Collins pbk £3.99
ISBN 0006718086

Ten funny stories follow one boy through school in a northern town in the 50s. All the funny situations and frustrations of childhood and adolescence - being in the right gang, fibs that get out of hand and trying to persuade your mum to buy you the right trousers. Lots of dialogue makes this an easy and entertaining read.
8-10

FOR THE LOVE OF A HORSE
Patricia Leitch
Collins pbk £2.99
ISBN 0006926533

There are 12 Jinny stories available. The first one 'For the Love of a Horse' tells how Jinny rescues a pure-bred Arab mare from a cruel circus to realise her dreams of owning her own horse. Sometimes the idyllic Scottish moorland life they share is troubled and this series explores their adventures together.
10-12

THE LION, THE WITCH AND THE WARDROBE
CS Lewis
Collins pbk £3.50
ISBN 0006716636

The first book to be written in the magical Narnia series. The four Pevensey children, stumble through the back of a wardrobe into the fantastical world of Narnia, which is in the grip of an evil white witch. Essential reading for imaginative children.
10-12

PIPPI LONGSTOCKING
Astrid Lindgren
Puffin pbk £3.75
ISBN 0140308946

Pippi, a remarkably strong young girl, lives a life without adults, that most can only dream of. With no one to answer to, she has a series of adventures that leaves the reader and her more conventional neighbours amazed and amused.
8-10

THE GHOST OF THOMAS KEMPE
Penelope Lively
Mammoth pbk £3.50
ISBN 0749707917

James' life is made a misery by a ghost. Not because Thomas Kempe is a creepy ghost, but because no-one believes that the banging, breaking of crockery and the rude messages aren't caused by a ten year old boy.
8-10

THE STORY OF DOCTOR DOLITTLE
Hugh Lofting
Red Fox pbk £3.99
ISBN 0099854600

Doctor Dolittle prefers the company of animals to that of humans, and does indeed talk to them. In the first story of a series the Doctor travels to Africa, and has a succession of extraordinary adventures.
8-10

ANASTASIA KRUPNIK
Lois Lowry
Collins pbk £2.99
ISBN 0006726356

Anastasia is an independent young girl who is given a degree of responsibility over her own life by her parents. In this book we see her discovering how she feels about babies, religion and old people. Good fun and easy to read.
8-10

BACK HOME
Michelle Magorian
Puffin pbk £4.99
ISBN 0140319077

Austere, post-war Britain comes as a terrible shock to Rusty after five years as an evacuee in affluent America with a caring, easy-going foster family. Rusty needs every ounce of her indomitable spirit to cope with a stern and distant family and a new school deeply hostile to her American accent and ways. A deeply satisfying book with an outspoken heroine who won't ever learn to do the 'done thing'.
10-12

GOODNIGHT MR TOM
Michelle Magorian
Puffin pbk £4.99
ISBN 0140315411

When Willie Beech, an unloved and lonely evacuee, is billeted with Tom Oakley, a stubborn and equally solitary old man, they begin tentatively to form a bond of love both unexpected and unsought. When Willie is recalled to London and disappears, Tom is finally galvanised into action. A harrowing and powerful book.

☆ 10–12

THE HAUNTING
Margaret Mahy
Puffin pbk £3.50
ISBN 0140363254

Barney is frightened. He's being haunted, and the voice and the footsteps are getting closer. As much about a family as the supernatural, the eerie and claustrophobic atmosphere is balanced with great warmth and humour.

☆ 📖 10–12

WE HATE BALLET
Jahnna Malcolm
Collins pbk £2.99
ISBN 0006934013

Five misfit and mutinous young ballet dancers find their feet, and friendship, when they team up to face whatever horrors the corps de ballet (and especially the 'bunheads') can throw at them. There are ten books so far in this very funny 'Scrambled Legs' series.

8–10

HANDLES
Jan Mark
Puffin pbk £3.99
ISBN 014031587X

Sent to stay with her dismal aunt and family where she feels utterly displaced, Erica finds new friends and a sense of normality among the Mercury Motorcycles where everyone who belongs has a 'handle' or nickname.

☆ 10–12

THUNDER AND LIGHTNINGS
Jan Mark
Puffin pbk £3.75
ISBN 0140310630

Moving to East Anglia, Andrew's scatty and intellectual family is adopted by Victor, a wilful and ill-educated but remarkably astute young neighbour. Andrew is glad of the new friendship, but

Victor is disconsolate at the impending decommissioning of his beloved Lightning aeroplanes.

☆ 📖 10–12

WALKABOUT
James Vance Marshall
Puffin pbk £3.50
ISBN 0140312927

Sole survivors of a plane crash in the Australian desert, Mary and her younger brother Peter will certainly die, but then an Aboriginal boy finds them and teaches them to survive in the outback, giving them the spirit to survive and go on even after his own death.

10–12

THE BABYSITTERS CLUB
Ann M Martin
Scholastic pbk £1.99 – £2.50

Stories from the members of the Babysitters Club, told in their own voices, about the fun, the trials and the tribulations of pre-teenage life and serious babysitting.

8–10

Philip Ridley

Philip Ridley cites influences as diverse as fairy stories, Dickens, Marvel comics and Spielberg movies. The resulting fiction explodes onto the page – an amazing amalgam of addictive storytelling, dazzling characterisation and dialogue to die for!

His triumph is to win fans in both readers and critics. He was chosen by children as the winner of the Mind Boggling Books Award and has also been shortlisted for the prestigious Whitbread Award.

He confronts tough issues (homelessness, family breakdown) with imagination and humour. Observer cartoonist Chris Riddell illustrates his novels and the Guardian has said 'Ridley and Riddell have created something of a new genre'.

Philip Ridley is an artist, a novelist, a playwright and screen writer and a movie producer! However, he says:

'My children's books are the backbone of everything I do. They are where I explore the thing I'm mainly interested in, which is pure storytelling.'

Some books by Philip Ridley
Meteorite Spoon
Kasper in the Glitter
Dakota of the White Flats
(all published by Puffin)

THE BOX OF DELIGHTS
John Masefield
Mammoth pbk £3.99
ISBN 0749712864

When Kay meets a mysterious Punch and Judy man, he becomes involved in a strange and thrilling adventure. Evil Abner Brown and his dangerous wolves will do anything to obtain the magical box, and only Kay can stop them. A brilliantly exciting story unfolds ...

10–12

LOW TIDE
William Mayne
Red Fox pbk £3.50
ISBN 0099183110

The low tide precedes a devastating tidal wave which picks up three children and abandons them high in the interior of New Zealand's South Island where, alone with their fears and legends, they must find a way back home.

☆ 10–12

RUN WITH THE WIND
Tom McCaughrean
Puffin pbk £3.99
ISBN 014034487X

The captivating story of life in the wild for a skulk of foxes. The fox family under-take a dangerous journey to find the secret of survival. Charming line drawings complement the text.
Irish edition by Wolfhound Press
ISBN 0863270719

10–12

THE GREAT SMILE ROBBERY
Roger McGough
Puffin pbk £3.25
ISBN 0140314377

How can Emerson win the smiling competition and cheer up the world when the terrible stinkers have stolen all his special smiles and are wearing them all wrong? Very funny.

8–10

THE EXILES
Hilary McKay
Collins pbk £3.50
ISBN 0006746438

Big Grandma thinks her eccentric and headstrong grand-daughters do too much reading and not enough living, so when they are sent, under duress, to stay with her, a ban on reading produces some extraordinary results.

☆ 10–12

WINNIE THE POOH
AA Milne
Mammoth pbk £4.99
ISBN 0749707100

All-time classic favourites, these stories of Christopher Robin and his bear, not to mention Piglet, Eeyore, Owl and Rabbit, are an intrinsic part of most childhoods. Funny and quirky, they are excellent for reading aloud to younger children. More gentle adventures in 'The House at Pooh Corner'. Gift editions available.

📖 8–10

ANNE OF GREEN GABLES
LM Montgomery
Puffin pbk £2.99
ISBN 0140367411

The first, and best-known of the ten books about vivacious Anne Shirley, a red-haired orphan who invades the lives of a quiet Canadian farming family. Drawn from the author's real life experiences with her grandparents on Prince Edward Island at the end of the last century.

📖 10–12

DOUBLE IMAGE
Pat Moon
Orchard pbk £3.99
ISBN 1852137614

When his cold, remote Nan Robinson dies, David feels no grief. Then he finds an old photograph of a boy, with his face, and as he unravels the family secrets behind it, he begins to understand ...
Compassionate and compelling.

10–12

Now We Are Six P.95

THE WRECK OF THE ZANZIBAR
Michael Morpurgo
Mammoth pbk £2.99
ISBN 0749726202

In 1907 Laura decides to keep a diary. In 1995 her great nephew reads it and relives her experiences. A beautiful, but tragic tale of poverty and hope.
 8–10

WHY THE WHALES CAME
Michael Morpurgo
Mammoth pbk £3.50
ISBN 074970537X

When a whale is beached, Gracie and Daniel think it deserves to live. The one

person to share their view is the Birdman. Their joint battle to save the whale results in the children finding out more about the mysterious Birdman. An unusual tale.
10–12

REBECCA'S WORLD
Terry Nation
Red Fox pbk £2.99
ISBN 099463903

Rebecca's problem is that she is bored. This is soon solved for her, when she is transported to another planet; now her problem is getting home. A funny and exciting fantasy story.
8–10

THE GOALKEEPER'S REVENGE AND OTHER STORIES
Bill Naughton
Puffin pbk £3.50
ISBN 0140303480

This is a delightful and lively collection of stories. Ranging from the comic (Timothy) to the tragic (Spit Nolan), Naughton takes the reader through the gamut of human emotion.
8–10

MY MATE SHOFIQ
Jan Needle
Collins pbk £2.99
ISBN 0006715184

Bernard confesses to witnessing an attack and soon realises what the effects of honesty can be. A realistic portrayal of a sensitive issue.
10–12

FIVE CHILDREN AND IT
E Nesbit
Puffin pbk £3.50
ISBN 0140301283

Five children try to dig their way to Australia – and find a Psammead (also known as a sand fairy) instead. This strange and rather ugly creature grants them 5 wishes but things don't turn out quite as anticipated.
10–12

THE RAILWAY CHILDREN
E Nesbit
Puffin pbk £2.50
ISBN 0140366717

Roberta, Peter and Phyllis find their lives turned upside-down when their father has to go away unexpectedly. Leaving their London home, they move away to a small house near a railway line, which is to have a significant influence on them. A touching story, which has been loved for nearly 100 years.
10–12

The Way to Sattin Shore

THE BORROWERS
Mary Norton
Puffin pbk £3.99
ISBN 014036451X

Pod, Homily, and Arietty
are borrowers – a race of
tiny people who borrow
everything they need from
'Human Beans', who don't
even know they exist. Then
Arietty changes everything
by making friends with the
boy upstairs. A story full of
wit, fun and imagination –
and as good an explanation
as any for what happens to
all those safety pins that 'just
disappear'.
🔖 8–10

MRS FRISBY AND THE RATS OF NIMH
Robert C O'Brien
Puffin pbk £3.99
ISBN 0141307257

It is time for the family of
mice to move to their winter
home, but poor Timothy
is too ill to be moved. Time
is running out for Mrs Frisby
and she is grateful for
any help she can get. An
easy to read, and funny
adventure story.
☆ 🔖 10–12

Z FOR ZACHARIAH
Robert O'Brien
Collins pbk £3.99
ISBN 0006710816

Ann has to come to terms
with being the sole survivor
of a nuclear holocaust.
However, her solitude is
interrupted by an apparent-
ly sinister man. The book
takes the form of Ann's

diary and is both mysterious
and compassionate.
10–12

Francine Pascal

*The tremendously popular
Sweet Valley Series now follows
the identical Wakefield twins
from the age of 7, in 'Sweet
Valley Kids', right through to
college years in 'Sweet Valley
University'. Compulsive, easy
to read, and featuring issues
relevant to the age group.*

BEST FRIENDS
Francine Pascal
Transworld pbk £2.99
ISBN 0553173758

The first book in the
'Sweet Valley Twins' series.
Elizabeth and Jessica may
appear identical, but they
view the world very
differently. Elizabeth
wants to start a newspaper,
whilst Jessica is more
interested in being popular.
10–12

BRIDGE TO TERABITHIA
Katherine Paterson
Puffin pbk £3.50
ISBN 0140366180

A startling novel in which a
secret country is created in
the woods. It offers hope
and solace, but is that
enough? Hugely enjoyable,
with an unexpected plot.
☆ 10–12

TOM'S MIDNIGHT GARDEN
Philippa Pearce
Puffin pbk £4.50
ISBN 0140364544

Philippa Pearce has a repu-
tation for crafting beautiful
stories into modern classics,
and this book is quite outstanding. Staying with his
aunt and uncle isn't what
Tom had planned for his
summer holidays, but there
are some surprises in store
for Tom when he hears the
old clock strike 13. A lovely
and memorable story with
a moving conclusion.
🔖 10–12

THE WAY TO SATTIN SHORE
Philippa Pearce
Puffin pbk £3.99
ISBN 0140316442

This highly enjoyable book
sees Kate searching for
answers to her family's
secretive past. Whether Kate
can cope with the answers
to her questions propels the
reader to the end of this
exceptional story.
🔖 10–12

HENRY'S LEG
Anne Pilling
Puffin pbk £3.50
ISBN 0140329781

Finding the leg of a fashion
dummy is how Henry's
troubles begin. The local
gang of thugs want to have
the leg back. The perfect
book to discourage 'junk
hoarders' and a funny
adventure story too!
☆ 🔖 10–12

ARCTIC ADVENTURE
Willard Price
Red Fox Pbk £3.50
ISBN 0099183218

In freezing temperatures, and with dwindling food supplies, wild animals are not all that the boys have to contend with ... This is part of a popular adventure series, in which Hal and Roger travel the world to collect wild animals for their father's zoo.

10~12

MEMOIRS OF A DANGEROUS ALIEN
Maggie Prince
Orion pbk £3.99
ISBN 1858810736

It is the 21st Century and Dominic's neighbour is an alien – in fact, he soon finds out that the whole planet is overrun with them. But what are they after – information, domination, or are they just protecting their own world? Dominic has to find out who the enemy is, and save planet earth.

☆ 🔖 10~12

Meteorite Spoon

SWALLOWS AND AMAZONS
Arthur Ransome
Red Fox pbk £3.99
ISBN 009996290X

A wonderful escapist story of childhood adventure set in the Lake District. John, Susan, Titty and Roger spend the summer camping on Wild Cat Island. When the local Amazon pirates challenge the town children to prove their seamanship, the stakes are high. This is the first in a series of sailing adventures. These famous books are also available as beautiful gift edition hardbacks.

🔖 10~12

KRINDLEKRAX
Philip Ridley
Red Fox pbk £2.99
ISBN 0099979209

Skinny, knock-kneed Ruskin wants to be the hero in the school play – but so does the school bully. Things don't look good until the discovery of a monster in the sewers, and Ruskin proves himself a hero after all.

☆ 🔖 8~10

METEORITE SPOON
Philip Ridley
Puffin pbk £3.99
ISBN 0140368906

After their parents have a cataclysmic row, Filly and Fergal discover the land of Honeymoonia, with the aid of a magic spoon. There they meet a couple just like

their parents – but the two never have a cross word.

8~10

GRIZZLY TALES FOR GRUESOME KIDS
Jamie Rix
Puffin pbk £3.50
ISBN 0140345728

Cautionary tales were originally intended to chasten children into good behaviour. While it is unlikely that they will have an improving effect, kids will certainly relish these stories of disobedient children and their sticky, horrid ends.

🔖 8~10

Puzzle Adventures

These are good stories for reluctant readers requiring plenty of interaction throughout, with illustrated clues needing to be solved to work out the mysteries. The stories are available individually or in collections. Advanced Puzzle Adventures are also available.

CURSE OF THE LOST IDOL
Graham Round
Usborne pbk £3.50
ISBN 074600012X

In this story, Professor Pott and his assistant Eric discover the lost idol, which is cursed and must be protected.

8~10

ESCAPE FROM BLOOD CASTLE
Graham Round
Usbourne pbk £3.50
ISBN 0860209504

Intrepid Ivor ventures into Blood Castle to prevent himself from being cheated out of his wealth and title by his cousin 'The Baron'.

8–10

THE SILVER SWORD
Ian Serrallier
Puffin pbk £4.50
ISBN 0140364528

Based on a true story, this wonderful book tells of the struggle of four children trying to keep alive during the Nazi occupation of Poland, and of their search for their parents after the war ends. A compulsive read.

📖 10–12

BLACK BEAUTY
Anna Sewell
Puffin pbk £2.50
ISBN 0140366849

Perhaps best known and best-loved of all animal stories, Black Beauty was originally written to highlight the cruel way horses were treated last century. A dramatic story of misfortune and eventual happiness which still appeals to the tender-hearted today.

10–12

Shakespeare for Children

These books all adopt very different approaches, but are written with the aim of making Shakespeare accessible to children without losing the essence of the original works. All are superb adaptations.

SHAKESPEARE - THE ANIMATED TALES
Leon Garfield
Heinemann pbk £15.00
ISBN 0434962287

Beautifully illustrated in cartoon style and adhering to the format of a play, this book brings Shakespeare back to life visually, which, of course, is the best way to discover him. Comes with background notes and an introduction to Shakespearean theatre in general. Each individual tale also available at £4.99.

10–12

SHAKESPEARE'S STORIES VOLUME 1
Leon Garfield
Gollancz pbk £10.00
ISBN 0575043407

'Shakespeare Stories' are rewritten by the distinguished children's author in a more simplified manner, but with the inclusion of some of the original text. Stunning illustrations by the award winning Michael Foreman.

10–12

SHAKESPEARE WITHOUT THE BORING BITS
Humphrey Carpenter
Viking pbk £4.99
ISBN 0670855340

Humphrey Carpenter brings together some of Shakespeare's best known works and retells them as they have never been told before. Brought totally up to date, they are very accessible and humorous, reminding us how the themes of the plays are still relevant today.

10–12

The Silver Sword

CARBONEL
Barbara Sleigh
Puffin pbk £3.99
ISBN 0140301550

Rosemary and John must hurry to release Carbonel, the witch's cat, from his binding spell before full moon so that he can reclaim his rooftop kingdom. A magical story and a perennial favourite.

📖 8–10

Russell Stannard

'When I was young I was mad about cricket – I dreamed of becoming a famous player. I only did physics because the school laboratory overlooked the Oval cricket ground. But I never did get to play for England. Instead I got hooked on physics'.

Russell Stannard is a professor of Physics at the Open University. He's not scared of introducing children to demanding and complex subjects. His books discuss the Theory of Relativity, Black Holes and Quantum Leaps – subjects that most adults have trouble comprehending!

Einstein once said 'Common sense consists of that layer of prejudice laid down in the mind before the age of 18'.

Russell Stannard says 'Exactly! It 's a waste of time trying to put across such ideas to adults. It is children I ought to be addressing'.

The books are not just educational though, they are funny, fast-moving novels. One child said to Stannard 'What I like about your books is that they teach you interesting things without you knowing it'.

Books by Russell Stannard:

The Time and Space of Uncle Albert
Black Holes and Uncle Albert
Uncle Albert and Quantum Quest

Here I am!
World of 1001 Mysteries
Letters to Uncle Albert
(available in April 1996)
(all published by Faber)

101 DALMATIANS
Dodie Smith
Mammoth pbk £3.99
ISBN 0749702044

Dogs of every kind, from far and wide, help Pongo and Missis rescue their puppies from the clutches of Cruella de Vil. An animal adventure that's hard to beat. Ladybird publish versions of the Disney movie for younger children.

 10–12

THE FANTASTIC MAZE BOOK
Juliet and Charles Snape
Julia MacRae pbk £3.99
ISBN 1856810097

This book was an immediate success on publication. The ingenious mazes take you through doors, down tunnels and up ropes and each beautifully illustrated double page is a whole world to pore over. Explore castles, forests, pirate ships and more.

10–12

THE LITTLE VAMPIRE
Angela Sommer-Bodenburg
Scholastic pbk £2.99
ISBN 0590555979

Tony, an avid fan of horror films and monster books, finds an intruder in his room one night – an intruder with red eyes and pointed teeth. The little vampire turns out to be less ferocious than he looks but when Tony's parents hear he has a new friend, they invite him around for tea …

8–10

HEIDI
Johanna Spyri
Puffin pbk £2.99
ISBN 0140366792

Heidi, a 5 year old orphan, learns to love life in the Alps with her grandfather. Both are heartbroken when she is sent to live in Frankfurt with another family but she eventually learns to love them both. A lovely story full of wonderful characters. Also available in hardback.

8–10

Russell Stannard

Described by the Times Educational Supplement as 'a breath of scientific fresh air', Stannard is a relatively new author who combines being professor of physics at the Open University with writing novels designed to make science and other 'big' issues accessible and entertaining. Stannard will undoubtedly provoke difficult questions and inspire children to find out more.

THE TIME & SPACE OF UNCLE ALBERT
Faber pbk £3.99
ISBN 0571142826

Uncle Albert and his niece Gedanken explore the peculiarities of time and space by means of an imaginary space ship. Science made simple and fun!

 10–12

BLACK HOLES & UNCLE ALBERT
Faber pbk £3.99
ISBN 0571144535

'If you were falling into a black hole with a clock, would the hands stop?' Find out when our heroes visit the moon, go for space walks and discover the stars.

10–12

The Little Vampire

UNCLE ALBERT AND THE QUANTUM QUEST
Faber pbk £3.99
ISBN 0571173446

The last Uncle Albert adventure sees Gedanken shrinking like Alice in Wonderland to explore the world of jumping quarks and electrons. A quiz at the end checks how much you've understood.

10–12

Goosebumps

- R.L. Stine started his career writing funny books under the pseudonym Jovial Bob!
- He receives 500 letters a week from Goosebumps fans
- American readers campaigned this year to change Halloween to Goosebumps Day!

TREASURE ISLAND
RL Stevenson
Puffin pbk £2.99
ISBN 0140366725

High seas, tall ships, pirates and hidden treasure, memorable characters like Blind Pew and Long John Silver. Cabin boy Jack Hawkins survives all and wins out. A classic tale which still excites today. Available in many other versions from Ladybird to hardback gift edition.

10–12

WELCOME TO THE DEAD HOUSE
RL Stine
Scholastic pbk £2.99
ISBN 0590553089

Imagine having to move to a huge creepy house in a dark gloomy town – then finding you're not alone. First book in the phenomenally popular and readable 'Goosebumps' series.

8–10

MARIANNE DREAMS
Catherine Storr
Puffin pbk £3.99
ISBN 0140302093

Marianne is bored, recovering in bed from an illness. She begins to draw, and the drawings find their way into sinister dreams, where a boy is trapped in a prison of her making.

10–12

BALLET SHOES
Noel Streatfield
Puffin pbk £4.25
ISBN 0140364595

Warm and involving story of three very different girls, adopted at birth by an eccentric and largely absent professor. Definitely not just for ballet fanatics – the experiences of the Fossils at the Academy of Dance and their determination to make a mark on the world will delight many readers.

10–12

THE EAGLE OF THE NINTH
Rosemary Sutcliff
Puffin pbk £4.99
ISBN 0140364579

A soldier sets off on a dangerous journey, north of Hadrian's wall, to discover the truth about the disappearance of an entire Roman Legion. Can he solve the mystery and find the Eagle, symbol of the legion's honour?

10–12

SUN HORSE, MOON HORSE
Rosemary Sutcliff
Red Fox pbk £2.99
ISBN 0099795604

Magical tale of an early Iron Age tribe, of Lubrin's efforts to save them, and of the White Horse of Uffington's origins.

10–12

DRACULA'S CASTLE
Robert Swindells
Transworld pbk £2.50
ISBN 0440862787

Twins Sam and Laura are suspicious when they see a classmate sneaking into a deserted old house nicknamed Dracula's Castle, and become even more curious when he starts to feel ill and miss school. What is the secret of the old house? The twins investigate and find a very unusual vampire who can only be got rid of through very unusual tactics.

8–10

Dracula's Castle

ROOM 13
Robert Swindells
Transworld pbk £2.99
ISBN 0440862272

Vampires and other spooky creatures abound in this frightening tale of Fliss's school trip to Whitby. Unputdownable!

10-12

THE CAY
Theodore Taylor
Puffin pbk £3.50
ISBN 0140305955

Philip, a young white boy and Timothy, an old black Jamaican man are shipwrecked. This touching story describes Philip's ability to come to terms with his sudden blindness and the development of the friendship between the two characters.
📖 10-12

THE RUNAWAYS
Ruth Thomas
Red Fox pbk £3.50
ISBN 0099596601

Misfits at school and not very happy at home, Julia and Nathan happen to stumble upon a large sum of money and are forced to run away with it. So begins an adventure that has incredible highs and lows and leaves them both very different people. A compelling and involving story.
☆ 10-12

THE SECRET
Ruth Thomas
Red Fox pbk £3.50
ISBN 0099840006

Nicky and Roy's mum doesn't come home after a weekend away and they are too scared to tell the authorities. Their determination to cope on their own and to get their mum back is a triumph over circumstances. Thomas writes with real sympathy and understanding for her complex characters.

10-12

MARY POPPINS
PL Travers
Collins pbk £3.99
ISBN 0006747876

The first book about Mary Poppins, the magical and mischievous nanny with a veneer of respectability. She changes the lives of Jane and Michael Banks for ever by whisking them off to fantastic worlds.

10-12

PIGEON SUMMER
Ann Turnbull
Walker pbk £3.99
ISBN 0744530814

Mary loves her father's racing pigeons just as much as he does. But it is 1930, her father has to leave in search of work, and there's barely enough money for bread, never mind pigeon feed. The tension between Mary and her mother mounts ...

10-12

PONGWIFFY
Kaye Umansky
Puffin pbk £3.50
ISBN 0140342214

The funny story about a smelly witch and her quest to outshine other witches. A very readable book with a brilliant collection of characters.
📖 8-10

A TRAVELLER IN TIME
Alison Uttley
Puffin pbk £3.99
ISBN 0140309314

While staying with her Great Aunt in her old, atmospheric farmhouse, Penelope finds herself slipping back in time to the politically volatile Elizabethan age. As she becomes more involved with the Babington family, and the doomed plan to save Mary, Queen of Scots, the sense of tragedy increases, for she holds the awful knowledge of what will happen.

10-12

AROUND THE WORLD IN 80 DAYS
Jules Verne
Puffin pbk £3.50
ISBN 014036711X

One of Jules Verne's three timeless classics in which Phileas Fogg and his comic valet Passepartout undertake an incredible journey.

10-12

Sylvia Waugh

Sylvia Waugh (say 'Woff') was born and has lived most of her life in Gateshead. She was a teacher for many years and although she has been a compulsive writer since childhood, it wasn't until she retired that she published her first novel. 'The Mennyms' was published in 1993 to great literary acclaim and won The Guardian Fiction award.

'I haven't got any dogmatic theory on children's books. There are all sorts around. Some I like and some I don't. And that's the way it should be. Children, like grown-ups, have a wide variety of tastes. When I was teaching, the best bit was always reading to a class something that I like myself, and feeling that I was sharing the pleasure.'

WHAT OTHERS SAY ABOUT THE MENNYMS:

'Woven into the fabric of this weird, witty and wonderfully original story are some wry observations of family life, and some haunting reflections on the nature of reality which make you want to read it all over again' *The Guardian*

'It is an extraordinary book, quite unlike anything else that has been written for years. When you reach the end you have become so engrossed in a story about rag dolls, set almost entirely within the confines of a suburban house, but you do not doubt that you have just read a classic' *Sunday Telegraph*

Books by Sylvia Waugh

THE MENNYMS

THE MENNYMS IN THE WILDERNESS

THE MENNYMS UNDER SIEGE

(Published by Julia MacRae and Red Fox)

NAPPER GOES FOR GOAL
Martin Waddell
Puffin pbk £3.25
ISBN 0140313184

Perfect for football fans –
full of tactics and explanatory
diagrams, as well as likeable
characters, humour, and a
good yarn. First in a series.

8–10

PARCEL OF PATTERNS
Jill Paton Walsh
Puffin pbk £3.50
ISBN 0140362592

Based on the true story of
the devastating effects of
plague on the Derbyshire
village of Eyam, and the
courageous response of its
inhabitants, this is also the
story of a young girl's personal act of self sacrifice.

10–12

THE MENNYMS
Sylvia Waugh
Red Fox pbk £2.99
ISBN 0099301679

Strange tale of the Mennym
family, who try so hard to be
ordinary. Their quiet lives
are threatened by a letter
that heralds a visit from
abroad – and if Albert Pond
sets eyes upon them, he'll
know they're not like other
folk at all.

☆ 10–12

BLITZCAT
Robert Westall
Macmillan pbk £3.50
ISBN 0330310402

Powerfully written, some-
times grim story of a cat

travelling through the Blitz
in search of her master.
Through her and the cast
of ordinary people she
encounters, the reader feels
a very real sense of the loneliness, horror and sudden
intimacies of war time.

☆ 10–12

THE MACHINE GUNNERS
Robert Westall
Macmillan pbk £3.99
ISBN 033033428X

Chas McGill collects war
souvenirs, so when a German
plane crashes with the
machine gun still intact, he
is determined to have it. But
in such violent times, he and
his friends cannot remain
content with being onlookers
and collectors – they want a
piece of the action.

☆ 📖 10–12

CHARLOTTE'S WEB
EB White
Puffin pbk £3.99
ISBN 1040301852

The funny, tender story of a
pig called Wilbur and his
friend Charlotte's clever
campaign to save him from the
inevitable fate of a plump pig.

8–10

THE SWORD IN THE
STONE
TH White
Collins pbk £3.99
ISBN 0006742009

A magical story set in an
England before Arthur
becomes King. Teeming
with magicians, giants,

knights and witches, it is
a delight to read.

10–12

DOWN CAME A
BLACKBIRD
Nicholas Wilde
Collins pbk £3.50
ISBN 0006746772

When troubled, defensive
James is sent to live with his
great uncle, in a house which
resonates with secrets, echoes
of the past begin to find their
way into his dreams. Tense
and emotionally charged.

10–12

LITTLE HOUSE IN THE BIG
WOODS
Laura Ingalls Wilder
Mammoth pbk £3.99
ISBN 0749709316

First in a series of books
about a pioneering child-
hood spent travelling across
America 120 years ago,
through land shared with
bears and wolves. Beautifully
written, and all the more
captivating because it is true.

10–12

TARKA THE OTTER
Henry Williamson
Puffin pbk £4.99
ISBN 0140366210

An atmospheric, richly
detailed story of an otter
and her cubs and their daily
struggle for survival. Ideal
reading for all lovers of animals and the countryside.

10–12

GETTING RICH WITH JEREMY JAMES
David Henry Wilson
Macmillan pbk £2.99
ISBN 0330283839

A series of stories featuring young Jeremy James who, amongst other things, attempts to get rich, drive a car and understand the logic behind a christening. An entertaining child's-eye view of an often nonsensical adult world.

〝〞 8–10

THE BED & BREAKFAST STAR
Jacqueline Wilson
Transworld pbk £2.99
ISBN 0440863244

Forced to move into a run-down bed and breakfast hotel with her family, Elsa keeps her spirits up with an endless stream of jokes. Although she frequently tries the patience of her adult companions, the true value of this engaging heroine finally shines through.

☆ 〝〞 8–10

THE STORY OF TRACY BEAKER
Jacqueline Wilson
Transworld pbk £2.50
ISBN 0440862795

Tracy Beaker lives in a children's home, where she decides to write her life story, in her own irrepressible style – wickedly observant and deeply touching.

☆ 8–10

THE SUITCASE KID
Jacqueline Wilson
Transworld pbk £2.99
ISBN 0440863112

Ten-year-old Andy finds herself living out of a suitcase as she is shunted between her parents' new homes and families after their divorce. Moving and believable, but frequently funny.

☆ 〝〞 8–10

The Story of Tracy Beaker

Anthologies

A SACKFUL OF STORIES FOR EIGHT YEAR OLDS
ed Pat Thomson
Transworld pbk £2.99
ISBN 0552527297

Funny and imaginative stories from favourite authors including Ted Hughes, Penelope Lively and Russell Hoban. Ideal to read aloud too. Stories from 5 through to 9 years available.

FUNNY STORIES
ed Michael Rosen
Kingfisher pbk £4.99
ISBN 0862728010

A favourite volume from an excellent series - typically it mixes well known children's authors like Roald Dahl and Terry Jones, with tasters from James Thurber and Italo Calvino. Other titles include School Stories, Science Fiction Stories and Adventure Stories.

10–12

ORCHARD BOOK OF STORIES FROM THE BALLET
Geraldine McCaughrean
Orchard hbk £12.99
ISBN 1852134933

The stories of ten classic ballets are brought to life by the acclaimed storytelling skills of Geraldine McCaughrean and the bright but delicate illustrations of Angela Barrett.

8–10

THE HUTCHINSON TREASURY OF CHILDREN'S LITERATURE
ed Alison Sage
Hutchinson hbk £19.95
ISBN 0091761441

The essential family collection of classics old and new, from Mother Goose and Quentin Blake to Brian Jacques and Kenneth Grahame. Lavishly illustrated, often from the original texts, this will be an inviting first taste or a reminder of old favourites.

Poetry

Poetry

Chidren love poetry from an early age, partly because it is one of the first kinds of language that they learn. Nursery Rhymes and lullabies are read and sung to them from birth. It seems natural to continue to enjoy rhythmic language as part of the experience of learning to read.

Poetry for children has also enjoyed a renaissance in the last 20 years, partly due to the efforts of school teachers. The increased focus in schools has meant that published poetry for children has flourished and several generations have grown to love the absurd and anarchic works of poets like Roger McGough and Michael Rosen.

The range available is better than it has ever been and we have tried to pick the best of the more traditional poets like AA Milne as well as contemporary and vibrant works by performance poets like Jackie Kay and Benjamin Zephaniah.

All the best anthologies are here too and are the best way to hook children who are not already poetry fans.

A Red Poetry Paintbox
Previous page: The Owl & the Pussycat P.94

Anthologies

FIRST POEMS
ed Julia Eccleshare
Orchard hbk £8.99
ISBN 1852134119

This collection will delight all young children. Bright and colourful pictures by Selina Young

The Walker Book of Poetry for Children

accompany a text which includes well-loved classics by writers like Robert Louis Stevenson and enjoyable surprises by less familiar names. An ideal gift to encourage a love of poetry for any first reader.
5–8

A VERY FIRST POETRY BOOK
ed John Foster
Oxford UP pbk £3.50
ISBN 0199160503

A book that is packed with easy to read poems about family, games, animals and monsters. The illustrations are bold and fun. This collection of poetry for the very young is the first in a series of titles which a child can follow as they grow.
5–8

THE WALKER BOOK OF POETRY FOR CHILDREN
ed Jack Prelutsky
Walker hbk £14.99
ISBN 0744502241

Jack Prelutsky is arguably America's leading children's poet with over thirty collections to his name and the anthology he has compiled is a sumptuous treasury of more than 500 poems. This beautifully designed hardback, with both black and white and colour illustrations by Arnold Lobel, is one of the best introductions to poetry a child could receive.

BOOK OF 20TH CENTURY VERSE
ed Brian Patten
Puffin pbk £6.99
ISBN 0140322361

Probably the definitive anthology of twentieth century poetry for children. The book starts with contemporary poets and moves back to the beginning of the twentieth century. The reader is taken on a journey through time – and poetry – from John Agard and Michael Rosen to Walter De La Mare and Thomas Hardy.
8–10

John Foster

John Foster's poetry anthologies for children, published by Oxford University Press, present children with original and contemporary poetry. Contributors to his books include Wendy Cope, Roger McGough and Ted Hughes. He has produced over 50 anthologies and also writes his own poetry.

'... a child centred, illustrated anthology which has proved irresistible.'

(*Child Education* on 'A First Poetry Book')

How did you first get your poems published?

... my first published collection was with the Oxford University Press when I edited a series of books including 'A First Poetry Book'. The idea was to present a collection of poetry for primary schools where some of the poems were about similar themes or ideas, but different poets approached them in contrasting ways. If you look carefully at some early editions you may find a few poems by someone called Derek Stuart, but actually he's a pseudonym for me!

When do you write poetry and what's your advice for young poets?

'I write ANYWHERE; sometimes at home, on the beach ... People who write poetry need to read lots of poetry ... the most important thing is to be prepared to struggle and fight for the right word or phrase. If you're stuck, it's a good idea to put the poem aside, then go back to it the following day.

'Become a word hoarder. Collect words and play with them – juggle with them, try out unusual combinations – stretch them and twist them 'till they say whatever you want them to say.'

I LIKE THIS POEM
ed Kaye Webb
Puffin pbk £4.99
ISBN 0140312951

This deservedly popular anthology, compiled by a former editor of Puffin Books, was the first to ask children to nominate their own poems for inclusion. The result is an eclectic choice that combines the traditional with the contemporary.

8–10

KINGFISHER BOOK OF CHILDREN'S POETRY
ed Michael Rosen
Kingfisher pbk £3.99
ISBN 0862727847

"What you have in this book", says Michael Rosen, "are hundreds of thoughts, dreams and ideas trapped in words for you to read, say or sing." The result is an anthology that gives excellent value, one crammed with old poems and new poems, sad poems and funny poems, with ballads, lyrics, riddles and nonsense verse.

WONDERCRUMP POETRY
ed Jennifer Curry
Red Fox pbk £3.99
ISBN 0099522616

Lively anthology collecting together the best entries in the Roald Dahl Foundation Poetry competition held every year. Written by poets of all ages from 4 - 17, and covering a wide range of subjects, these poems give an insight into what growing up today is like.

KINGFISHER BOOK OF COMIC VERSE
ed Roger McGough
Kingfisher pbk £3.99
ISBN 0862727855

Roger McGough's personal selection of comic verse is designed to provoke both the belly-laugh and the quiet smile, to incorporate all kinds of verse from the witty to the downright daft. Any anthology which can accommodate both Ezra Pound and Monty Python is bound to include something for every taste.

The Kingfisher Book of Comic Verse

'A sea-serpent saw a big tanker,

Bit a hole in her side and then sank her.

It swallowed the crew

In a minute or two,

And then picked its teeth with the anchor.'

Puffin Book of Twentieth Century Children's Verse

PENGUIN BOOK OF NONSENSE VERSE
ed Quentin Blake
Penguin pbk £9.99
ISBN 0140587578

A riotous and absurd feast of nonsense, compiled by Quentin Blake and illustrated in his unique style. Edward Lear and Lewis Carroll are present, of course, to introduce the reader to the Jumblies, the Ahkond of Swat and the Jabberwock. Other writers ask such important questions as 'Have You Ever Eaten Poodle Strudel' and warn against the dangers of bathing in Irish stew

A CARIBBEAN DOZEN
ed John Agard and Grace Nichols
Walker hbk £12.99
ISBN 0744521726

An uplifting collection of 13 poets from the Caribbean. Children will love the rich rhythms of the verse and enjoy the encounters with exotic animals such as pum na-na frogs and the zobo bird, with steel bands and with tropical fruits, with a world in which, "English nursery rhymes and fairy tales mingle with the tricky doings of Anancy Spiderman".

POETRY JUMP UP
ed Grace Nichols
Puffin pbk £3.50
ISBN 014034053X

A spirited and rich collection of some of the best Black poetry from around the world, from the Caribbean and Asia to Britain. An important collection, compiled by one of today's top black British writers, that introduces children to new sounds, rhythms, ideas and words expressed through poetry.
8–10

THIS POEM DOESN'T RHYME
ed Gerard Benson
Puffin pbk £3.99
ISBN 0140342273

What distinguishes poetry from prose? Most children would say rhyme but Benson shows that unrhymed poetry can be exciting and entertaining. Including the work of a wide range of poets (Shakespeare and Milton alongside James Berry and Wendy Cope) this is an unusual and inspiring anthology.
8–10 ☆

NIFFS & WHIFFS
ed Jennifer Curry
Red Fox pbk £2.99
ISBN 0099846101

Peculiar pongs and scintillating scents are the subject of this rib-tickling collection of smelly poetry provided by such fragrant poets as John Betjeman and Michael Rosen.
8–10

POETRY PAINTBOX
ed John Foster
All Oxford UP pbk £3.50
ISBN 019916679X

A favourite series with both teachers and pupils, the

Penguin Book of Nonsense Verse

books carry children from nursery school and the Red book to primary school and the Blue book. There are poems about castles, poems about pirates and poems about animals. Indeed there are poems about so many subjects that the books make it easy to incorporate poetry into the school day.

IN TIME OF WAR
ed Anne Harvey
Puffin pbk £3.99
ISBN 0140325786

An unforgettable collection for young adults which includes poems by both the greatest war poets (Owen, Sassoon and Keith Douglas) and by many lesser-known but equally affecting writers. Together they provide insights into the devastation and despair created by both World Wars.
12+

I WOULDN'T THANK YOU FOR A VALENTINE
ed Carol Ann Duffy
Puffin pbk £3.99
ISBN 0140346325

A collection of contemporary women's poetry for the teenage reader. Poets from very different backgrounds and cultures, from Maya Angelou to Wendy Cope, from Jean Binta Breeze to UA Fanthorpe, express their own memories and address issues important to all women.
12+

REAL COOL: POEMS TO GROW UP WITH
ed Niall MacMonagle

Martello pbk £7.99
ISBN 1860230024

A wide ranging collection of poems by international poets, covering all areas of teenage angst. From Roger McGough's 'Discretion' to Dorothy Parker's 'Valentine', there is something for everyone in this book.
12+

The Poets

I DIN DO NUTTIN
John Agard
Red Fox pbk £2.99
ISBN 0099184516

The Guyanese award-winning poet has stepped into a child's shoes and skipped and hopped from one experience to another with a sense of adventure and fun.

PLEASE MRS BUTLER
Allan Ahlberg
Puffin pbk £3.50
0140314946

These witty and often poignant poems cover all aspects of primary school life, from gangs in the playground to the nit nurse, from never-ending projects to supply teachers. Parents, teachers and school children alike will recognise the pleasures and perils of their everyday life in this collection.
8–10

HEARD IT IN THE PLAYGROUND
Allan Ahlberg
Puffin pbk £3.50
ISBN 0140328246

This sequel to Please Mrs Butler was the winner of the Signal Poetry Award. Once again the collection takes school as its subject and invites you to meet the Mad Professor's Daughter, be amazed at the Longest Kiss Contest and, if you're a hard-pressed teacher, to sing the Mrs Butler Blues.
8–10 ☆

CAUTIONARY VERSES
Hilaire Belloc, illustrations Quentin Blake
Red Fox pbk £4.99
ISBN 0099295318

Meet Matilda (who told such lies it made one gasp and stretch one's eyes) and Maria (who pulled faces) – just two of the legendary characters in this ever popular collection of Belloc's comical mockery of Victorian manners.

Rhymes Around the Year

What are 'Colly Birds' and 'Gabriel Hounds'? Did you know that Jack & Jill were once known as 'Hjuki' and 'Bil' and that Father Christmas once dressed in Green?! More fascinating and ridiculous information abounds in 'The Barefoot Book of Rhymes around the Year' by Marc Vyvyan-Jones (£12.99)

Roald Dahl

Roald Dahl's poetry has all the ingredients which children love – wickedly funny images, brisk rhymes and surprising twists of language – and, of course, the hints of cruelty that characterise his fiction. 'Revolting Rhymes' consists of six traditional fairy tales retold in verse. In 'Dirty Beasts' Dahl creates a ghastly menagerie of creatures doing unmentionable things. 'Rhyme Stew', for older children, transforms familiar fables and rhymes into very funny and occasionally ribald verse. In all three books Quentin Blake's mischievous illustrations complement the poems perfectly.

REVOLTING RHYMES
Puffin pbk £4.99
ISBN 0140504230

RHYME STEW
Puffin pbk £3.50
ISBN 0140343652

DIRTY BEASTS
Puffin pbk £4.99
ISBN 0140504354

TWO'S COMPANY
Jackie Kay
Puffin pbk £3.50
ISBN 014036952X

An exciting and vigorous collection of poetry from the Scottish born Jackie Kay, expressed with a particular energy and ear for dialogue and character. Her poems cover a range of issues, from imaginary friends and a new baby in the house to the grim reality of bullying and racism.

8~10 ☆

THE OWL AND THE PUSSYCAT
Edward Lear, illustrations Louise Voce
Walker pbk £4.99
ISBN 0744531217

One of the best loved nonsense rhymes ever is marvellously enhanced by Louise Voce's simple and direct illustrations. The boat has never been so beautiful nor so pea-green, the land where the Bong-Tree grows is clearly a desirable holiday destination and the mystery of just what exactly a runcible spoon looks like is finally cleared up.
A complete nonsense verse from Edward Lear is available in hardback.
8~10

Colin McNaughton

McNaughton is well known for his entertaining children's verse as well as his storybooks. His poems are absurd mixtures of fantasy and reality; monsters, aliens, and giants abound. Some poems are scary, but most are mischievously funny.

THERE'S AN AWFUL LOT OF WEIRDOS IN OUR NEIGHBOURHOOD
Walker pbk £6.99
ISBN 0744513383

An ideal introduction to McNaughton's world of rather silly verse and pictures. It would be difficult not to enjoy the antics of such curious characters as Crazy Frankie, Nosy Porker and Lemmy the Diver. And hard not to warm to the alternative version of a traditional rhyme which begins 'Monday's child is red and spotty/ Tuesday's child won't use the potty'.

LUCKY
Roger McGough
Puffin pbk £3.50
ISBN 0140361723

McGough's unique irreverency and comic imagination never fails to please and made this collection a successful Waterstone's Book of the Month and a real favourite with children.
8~10

AN IMAGINARY MENAGERIE
Roger McGough
Puffin pbk £3.50
ISBN 0140327908

McGough's classic book of poetry is a delight to get the tongue twisted around. Full of marvellously unusual, imaginary creatures, the poems and drawings (by Tony Blundell) will entertain time and time again.
8~10

SILLY VERSE FOR KIDS
Spike Milligan
Puffin pbk £3.25
ISBN 0140303316

Spike Milligan's inspired nonsense appeals to most children and is particularly evident in his poems. 'Silly Verse for Kids' includes, amongst other gems, the story of the Bongaloo and a moving tribute to 'English Teeth, English Teeth/Shining in the Sun'.
8-10

WHEN WE WERE VERY YOUNG
A A Milne
Mammoth pbk £4.99
ISBN 0749711809

Milne's first, classic collection of verse for children, illustrated in colour by Ernest Shepard. In these pages Christopher Robin continues to go down to Buckingham Palace with Alice and continues to kneel at the foot of the bed. Generations of children have grown up on these delightful poems and generations will continue to do so.

NOW WE ARE SIX
A A Milne
Mammoth pbk £4.99
ISBN 0749711795

The cosy middle class world in which the books were written has long since changed beyond recognition and yet they continue to sell in large numbers and remain as popular as ever. The work of A A Milne has charmed adults and children for nearly 70 years. It does begin to look as if Christopher Robin will be six now for ever and ever.

Silly Verse for Kids

Brian Patten

Brian Patten is one of Britain's best known and best loved children's poets. His work ranges from the serious and profound to the wacky and outrageous. He was born in Liverpool and left school at 15 to work as a reporter. He began writing poetry at an early age and started his own poetry magazine 'Underdog'. He is the winner of many awards.

GARGLING WITH JELLY
Puffin pbk £3.50
ISBN 0140319042

Brian Patten's ability to mix the lyrical with the hilarious is seen at its best in this collection of verse. Turning the pages the reader encounters poems that range from The Bee's Last Journey to The Rose, an evocation of passing time, to the knockabout humour of The Saga of the Doomed Cyclist.
8~10

THAWING FROZEN FROGS
Puffin pbk £3.50
ISBN 0140342710

An outrageous collection of comic and serious poems, a sequel to the successful 'Gargling with Jelly'. In it you can meet the Teachercreature and the Utter Butter Nutter, learn about the strange disease called Schoolitis and discover why toads look much more serious than frogs.
8~10

THE HYPNOTISER
Michael Rosen
Collins pbk £3.50
ISBN 0006732615

Michael Rosen has established himself as one of our most talented and popular children's poets. The secret of his success is in his ability to view life from a child's perspective and write about what children do and think and laugh about. 'The Hypnotiser' is one of his best works.

HOT DOG AND OTHER POEMS
Kit Wright
Puffin pbk £2.99
ISBN 0140313362

Kit Wright is a poet who has the gift of exciting children's imagination through laughter. In this collection you can meet the two old ladies who get colly-wobbles on a street full of cobbles, the rabbit who's as sick as a parrot because he's lost his carrot and Uncle Laurie who can't stop saying sorry. Illustrated by Posy Simmonds.
8~10

TALKING TURKEYS
Benjamin Zephaniah
Puffin pbk £3.50
ISBN 0140363300

A first collection of children's poetry from the fast-talking, vibrant rap poet. These are powerful, stimulating and fun poems which tackle environmental and other issues without ever becoming solemn or pompous. In his lively rhythms Zephaniah delivers poems which speak directly to you.
8~10

Page opposite:
The Eyewitness Atlas of the World P.99

Talking Turkeys

PACIFIC O

Reference

Probable plate
margin

PHILIPPINE PLATE
PACIFIC PLATE

New
Ireland

BISMARCK SEA

Man3ro △
1830m

Mt. Ulawun △
2335m

△ 8940m

New Britian

△ Mt. Bagana
1999m

Solo

BISMARCK
RANGE

New
Guinea

▲ Mt. Wilhelm
4506m

New Britain Trench

SOLOMON SEA

△ 4036m

SOLOMON SEA

OWEN STANLEY
RANGE

ARAFURA SEA

Torres Strait

Coral Sea Basin

CORAL

CAPE YORK
PENINSULA

Great Barrier Reef

SEA

MOR
A

ARNHEM
LAND

Gulf of
Carpentaria

Victoria

KIMBERLEY
PLATEAU
▲ 914m

Flinders

TANAMI
DESERT

GREAT DIVIDING RANGE

T SANDY
ESERT

L. Mackay

MACDONNELL RANGES
1510m ▲

SIMPSON
DESERT

Great
Artesian
Basin

GIBSON DESERT

Mt. Olga ▲▲ Uluru
1069m   868m

▲ 16

AUSTRALIA

L. Eyre

GREAT VICTORIA
DESERT

-16m ▼

Darling

FLINDERS RANGES

L. Torrens

innacles
esert

NULLARBOR PLAIN

Murray

Great Australian
Bight

Mt. Kosciusko ▲
2230m
AUSTRALIAN ALPS

Bass Strait

Reference

There was a time when reference books were just an extension of school – strictly for homework. The transformation in non-fiction publishing in the last 15 years has revolutionised reference books as learning tools.

Much of this credit must go to Dorling Kindersley, who bring information to life through photographs, three-dimensions and cross-sections. Their first-class designs and stunning photography,

and their un-stuffy and experimental approach to non-fiction have led the way. Similarly Usborne's bright and affordable paperbacks and Scholastic's 'Horrible Histories' (with their jokey and readable tracts on previously dry subjects like the Vikings and the Tudors) offer a fresh and lively approach.

A Child's Book of Art

The range of subject matter available now is also mind-blowing. You can get children's books on everything from philosophy to art history as well as a superior choice on all the usual sub-jects that fascinate children, like insects, dinosaurs, astronomy and castles.

We have put together an ultimate 'home library' for you, with what we think are the most innovative, read-able and comprehensive guides to most subjects. Don't just keep them for homework.

The Illustrated
History of the World

The Waterstone's Home Library

General Reference

CHILDREN'S ILLUSTRATED ENCYCLOPAEDIA
Dorling Kindersley hbk **£25.00**
ISBN 0751350923

Presented in a way that is both appealing and accessible to children, this is one of the best encyclopaedias available. Each A-Z entry is a self-contained topic but the cross-referencing system encourages travel from one related entry to another. It is illustrated with thousands of photographs, drawings and diagrams, covers a multitude of subjects and is regularly updated.

8–10

KALEIDOSCOPES
Kingfisher hbk **£12.99**

A series of dazzlingly designed non-fiction books for the older child which includes titles on Music, Painting, Theatre, the Stars, Trees and Forests and many other subjects. Each book demands the active participation of the child in creating transformations of the illustrations and the text. There are pages to unfold, stickers to place correctly and hidden pages to explore in these innovative books.

8–12 ☆

EYEWITNESS SERIES
Dorling Kindersley hbk
£8.99 *each*

A vast series of reference titles covering a wide variety of subjects. Clear photographs and a great depth of information make these perfect additions to any library.

8–10

FIRST DISCOVERY SERIES
Moonlight hbk **£6.50** *each*

First Discovery is an extensive series covering animals, people and nature. Each book concentrates on one subject such as 'Babies', 'Time', 'Weather' and uses transparent overlays to alter the pictures and present what is hidden from normal view. The books are educational and fun, helping children to take an active role in what they are reading. For example in 'The Body' the overlays reveal muscles, nerves and bones. The main text consists of simple, short sentences and extra detail is given by pieces of text tucked in among the pictures.

5–8

EYEWITNESS ATLAS OF THE WORLD
Dorling Kindersley hbk **£14.99**
ISBN 0751351261

This innovative and hugely informative atlas provides a fresh look at the world in which we live. Each of the easy-to-read maps is based on the most up-to-date information and is surrounded by dozens of photographs and illustrations designed to widen the reader's knowledge. There are also detailed keyboxes and specially researched text.

8–10

Art

CHILD'S BOOK OF ART
Lucy Micklethwait
Dorling Kindersley hbk **£9.99**
ISBN 0751350702

A striking combination of words and pictures, this book uses fine reproductions of well-known and not so well-known paintings to illustrate a child's first words. Colours are represented by paintings by David Hockney, Picasso, Matisse and Lucas Cranach, the seasons by Monet, Van Gogh, Millais and Bruegel. The result is a charming and eye-opening book.

Dictionaries

MY FIRST OXFORD DICTIONARY
Oxford UP hbk **£7.99**
ISBN 0199102368

The perfect introduction to the world of words for children of five and upwards. Colourfully illustrated with examples of 1,500 words, definitions and simple grammar.

5–8

OXFORD PRIMARY SCHOOL DICTIONARY
Oxford UP hbk £5.99
ISBN 0199103356

With 25,000 easy-to-understand definitions this dictionary is a treasure trove of words for children of eight and upwards. There are hundreds of specially drawn illustrations to clarify meanings and thousands of phrases and sentences to give examples of words used in the correct context.

8~10

OXFORD STUDY DICTIONARY
Oxford UP pbk £4.99
ISBN 0199103127

An ideal dictionary to use at school and for exams. The 45,000 headword entries include ones for specialist GCSE vocabulary and there are also 5,000 encyclopedic entries which cover countries, major cities, notable people and characters from myths and legends.

10~12

The Most Amazing Pop-up Science Books

Some of the awards this book has won...

British Book Award for the Best Children's Book of the Year

Rhone Poulenc Prize for Children's Science Book

Selected as one of Waterstone's Top 25 of 1994

History

HISTORY OF BRITAIN & IRELAND
Christopher Wright
Kingfisher hbk £14.99
ISBN 1856970256

An excellent reference book which covers history from the earliest people to the present. It is divided into time periods and each begins with an 'at a glance' chronological guide to major events. The writing is vivid and covers details of daily life as well as historical events, whilst maps, photographs, paintings and scenic reconstructions illuminate the text beautifully.

8~10

HORRIBLE HISTORIES
Terry Deary
Scholastic pbk £3.50 - £6.99

Horrible Histories make history fun by leaving out the boring bits and concentrating on the exciting and occasionally nasty parts! The series is always informative as well as fun, the mix of text and cartoons just right. If you thought history was boring then read Horrible Histories and think again!

8~10

THE ILLUSTRATED HISTORY OF THE WORLD
Plantaganet Somerset Fry
Dorling Kindersley hbk £25.00
ISBN 0751351989

This is perhaps the most comprehensive and stimul-ating history book ever produced for children. Intended for a generation at home in the global village the book covers all periods of history in all parts of the world. 1066 and the Battle of Hastings are still here but so too are the Chola peoples of India and the Anasazi cliff dwellers of North America who were William the Conqueror's contemporaries.

Health

WHERE DID I COME FROM
ISBN 0330331132

WHAT'S HAPPENING TO ME
ISBN 0330331124
Peter Mayle
Pan pbk 5.99 each

These books cover the facts of life in a clear, uncomplicated way. Ideal for any child between 5 and 12, they are amusing and very readable.

UNDERSTANDING THE FACTS OF LIFE
Susan Meredith
Usborne pbk £6.95
ISBN 0860208516

A sane and direct book which tackles tricky subjects without fuss. The book is divided into two sections, one on Growing Up and one on Babies, and with its combination of humorous illustration and instructive diagrams, it should go a long way towards informing the young reader and relieving many of their anxieties.

Terry Deary

Terry Deary was born at a very early age, so long ago that he can't even remember. He does remember that he discovered he could write at the age of 13 - but it took him another twenty years to discover that he could get paid for it! He lives and writes in his home county of Durham where he enjoys local cricket, messing about with computers and watching black and white movies - anything rather than work!

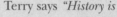

Terry says *"History is the world's longest-running soap opera. The drama, the action, the plots and, above all, the people - heroes and villains, clowns and killers. Horrible Histories tell tales of the crazy and the cruel, but the real stars are Mr and Mrs Ordinary who could have lived down your street in your town. I'm not a historian. I'm an actor turned story teller. People of the past are just the characters in my incredible but true soaps. Neighbours......from Hell!*

THE BLITZED BRITS

"Vulgar and remorselessly cheerful. History as spot on as this is not so much an account as an enactment" *Books for Keeps*

TERRIBLE TUDORS

"If you teach history you must have a copy. But keep it chained to the desk. Wet lunchtimes and end of term lessons will never be the same." *TES*

The Horrible Histories are published by Scholastic

HOW YOUR BODY WORKS
Usborne pbk £4.99
ISBN 0746023006

Where does food go? How do fingers work? How many bones do you have? These are three of the many questions answered by this entertaining but informative book which uses ingenious illustrations and everyday analogies that children will understand to explain the complicated functions of the body.

Science

MOST AMAZING POP-UP SCIENCE BOOK
Jay Young
Watts hbk £14.99
ISBN 0749614811

This unique example of the astonishing feats of paper engineering means that you can create working models to take you on a fascinating tour of scientific discovery. Hear a record play Edison's original recording, focus on minute details with the pop-up microscope and capture images on the screen of the camera obscura.

☆ 8-10

THE WAY THINGS WORK
David Macaulay
Dorling Kindersley hbk £17.99
ISBN 0863183239

Do you know what links a car tyre and a parachute? Did you know that the dentist's drill is a direct descendant of the first windmill? This break-through science book revolutionised the way machinery was explained to children. Fabulous illustrations clarify everything from the zipper to the microchip. A friendly mammoth provides the jokes.

8-10

USBORNE ILLUSTRATED DICTIONARY OF SCIENCE
Usborne pbk £9.99
ISBN 086020989X

Divided into three main branches of science – physics, chemistry and biology – this is a densely illustrated book which contains all the key concepts and terms. Thematically arranged so that words are defined in the context of related terms, the book also has a comprehensive index and is reliable both as a reference work and as a revision aid up to GCSE level.

10-12

INCREDIBLE CROSS-SECTIONS
Stephen Biesty
Dorling Kindersley hbk £12.99
ISBN 0863188079

Have you ever wanted to know where the toilets are in a space shuttle? Or maybe how many steps there are to the top of the Empire State Building? This fabulous book offers the opportunity to see inside 18 buildings and machines from a medi-aeval cathedral to a Spanish Galleon. Biesty's astonishingly detailed, cutaway illustrations take the reader into the hearts of his subjects.

8-10

Religion

THE CHILDREN'S ILLUSTRATED BIBLE
Dorling Kindersley hbk £15.99
ISBN 075135113X

In this magnificent new edition of the Bible all the best loved stories of both Old and New Testaments are retold by the well-known writer and reviewer Selina Hastings. Her fluent versions bring out the poetry and drama of the original while the vivid illustrations of Eric Thomas add an extra dimension to the book. Look out also for the Lion Children's Bible for slightly younger children.

WORLD RELIGIONS PAST AND PRESENT
Moonlight hbk £9.99
ISBN 1851030964

This comprehensive but compact book defines the core common to most religions; God, belief, prayer, festivals, death and mystery, good and evil. It also looks at religions in the Ancient World, the beliefs of the Egyptians, Greeks, Celts and others. The oral and written traditions of many living religions are also elucidated in a valuable and well illustrated volume.

Page opposite: Homecoming Pg.112

Young Adults

Young Adult

Adolescent readers are perhaps, the least likely to seek parental help when choosing books and yet at this stage, within reach of their adult reading lives they probably need more help and encouragement than ever.

We have selected a range of books that we consider to be excellent and hope will cover the interests of most 12 – 15 year olds. It ranges from Judy Blume's do-it-yourself growing up guides to Robert Cormier's bleak visions of the future, to the angst-ridden and comic Adrian Mole books. We have also included information on 'series' fiction and on teenage health guides.

Critics have often complained that books for this age group are too issue-based, and indeed many of them do deal with issues of sexuality, death, warfare, broken families etc. However most teenagers are forming their adult opinions at this age and these books help them explore their feelings in a safe and unembarrassing way.

Krindle Krax P.78

Finally, we have a few suggestions for the next step. Our further reading list offers a glimpse of the world of adult fiction now open to them.

A CREEPY COMPANY
Joan Aiken
Puffin pbk £4.50
ISBN 0140367896

A superb collection of spine-tingling supernatural tales. Take a ride down 'Dead Man's Lane', meet the creepy Mr Caspy and discover how Silence the Owl really died. Not for the faint-hearted.

I WAS A TEENAGE WORRIER
Ros Asquith
Transworld pbk £3.99
ISBN 0552140279

Introducing 15 year-old Letty Chubbis, typical teenage worrier, and her diary of angst

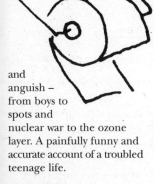

and anguish – from boys to spots and nuclear war to the ozone layer. A painfully funny and accurate account of a troubled teenage life.

MELUSINE
Lynne Reid Banks
Puffin pbk £4.50
ISBN 0140373330

A sensitive and sympathetic blend of mystery and fantasy which explores the troubled relationship between teenagers and parents, with a powerful and stunning conclusion.

ONE MORE RIVER
Lynne Reid Banks
Puffin pbk £4.99
ISBN 0140370218

The absorbing story of a young girl's struggle to adapt to her new life in an Israeli kibbutz, pulling together the fractured kaleidoscope of her personality while the world around her becomes enmeshed in the Arab-Israeli conflict.

TIGER EYES
Judy Blume
Pan pbk £3.50
ISBN 0330269542

Davey moves to New Mexico after her father is murdered during a raid on his store, and lives a life full of anger and resentment until she meets the mysterious Wolf, who shows her that life can begin again. A moving and keenly observed portrait of someone dealing with the death of a loved one.

FOREVER
Judy Blume
Pan pbk £3.99
ISBN 0330285335

Michael and Katharine's story of first love and first sex, still controversial due to its description of first sexual encounter. Almost a cult novel, it does offer some advice for young people just starting on the road to sexual independence.

DANCE ON MY GRAVE
Aidan Chambers
Red Fox pbk £3.99
ISBN 0099502917

A powerful, yet funny portrayal of a first homosexual relationship told in a thought-provoking mixture of story, reports, press cuttings, jokes and footnotes.

I was a Teenage Worrier

Aidan Chambers

Aidan Chambers started writing at the age of fifteen because, he says, he 'couldn't help it'. He spent 7 years as a monk where he discovered the value of silence, which, he says, 'helped him to become a better writer.'

GREGORY'S GIRL
Gerald Cole
Collins pbk £3.50
ISBN 0000672547

The overwhelming passion of Gregory's life is football, and things are thrown into turmoil when the stunning Dorothy joins his football team. A comedy of love and football based on the screenplay by Bill Forsyth.

NOT DRESSED LIKE THAT YOU DON'T!
Puffin pbk £3.50
ISBN 0140371788

EVERYBODY ELSE DOES! WHY CAN'T I?
Yvonne Coppard
Puffin pbk £3.99
ISBN 0140375392

Two hilarious diaries of a teenage girl and her mother. How will Cathy copy with her exams and her mother's mysterious behaviour? And how will her mother cope with the changing family?

Robert Cormier

Robert Cormier tackles contemporary teenage problems with uncompromising frankness. His powerful and sometimes disturbing novels often raise more questions than they answer and force readers to examine their own views of society and human nature.

AFTER THE FIRST DEATH
Collins pbk £3.99
ISBN 0006717055

Set high on a bridge in Massachusetts, this chilling study of bravery, cowardice, innocence and guilt revolves around a young terrorist's need to prove himself and examines the potential for evil in every one of us.

I AM THE CHEESE
Collins pbk £3.99
ISBN 0006717667

Adam's journey to visit his father in hospital becomes a sinister psychological odyssey. A gripping, but pessimistic thriller which examines the destruction of a young boy's mind under political interrogation.

THE CHOCOLATE WAR
Collins pbk £3.99
ISBN 0006717659

Cormier's best-known book is set in an American High School run by monks. It is a powerful exploration of individual struggle against brutal mob role and tells a bleak story of corruption, violence and the shocking abuse of power.

Everybody Else Does! Why Can't I?

CIRCLING THE TRIANGLE
Margrit Cruickshank
Poolbeg Press pbk £3.99
ISBN 1853711373

Stephen is in trouble at
home, at school, and above
all with the opposite sex.
Then the mysterious Ver
comes into his life and
suddenly things become
even more complicated.
A classic Irish teenage novel.

THE DIVORCE EXPRESS
Paula Danziger
Mammoth pbk £2.99
ISBN 0749723270

Phoebe spends over three
weeks a year riding on
buses, travelling between
her divorced parents' homes,
and feels that life is unfair.
A new friend helps her to
see that life can improve.
A cheerful and humorous
story about divorce.

THE CAT ATE MY GYMSUIT
Paula Danziger
Macmillan pbk £2.99
ISBN 0749723262

Marcy hates herself and
hates life. Her father is a
bully and school is a drag.
Ms Finney, the new English
teacher, gives her the confidence to stand up and be
counted. A revealing examination of how we perceive
ourselves, with an optimistic
ending.

THE CHANGES TRILOGY
Peter Dickinson
Puffin pbk £6.99
ISBN 0140318461

Peter Dickinson's terrifying
and gripping Changes
novels - The Devil's
Children, Heartsease, The
Weathermonger - in one
volume, set in a less-civilised
future England in which
machines have been over-
turned and people have
returned to primitive lives
of hardship and fear.

EVA
Peter Dickinson
Corgi pbk £3.99
ISBN 0552526096

13 year-old Eva wakes up in
hospital to discover that she
must live a new life - a life
that no-one has ever lived
before – in this gripping
examination of the possibilities and potential horrors of
medical experimentation.

AK
Peter Dickinson
Corgi pbk £2.99
ISBN 055252719X

Paul Kagomi is a boy soldier
fighting for freedom in the
African bush, with his AK47
rifle, the only thing he can
trust in a war-torn and
volatile situation. A compelling
and beautifully told story
of struggle and freedom.

DEAR NOBODY
Berlie Doherty
Collins pbk £3.99
ISBN 0006746187

Chris and Helen's teenage
lives are shattered when
Helen discovers she is
pregnant. Helen begins a
diary to the baby - Nobody -
and Chris writes his thoughts
in beautifully told and
revealing entries which
tell much about the fragile
nature of teenage lives
and loves.

GRANNY WAS A BUFFER GIRL
Berlie Doherty
Mammoth pbk £2.99
ISBN 074972384X

From her grandparents,
Hess hears the tale of Bridie
and Jack, of work as a buffer
girl in a cutlery factory and
her own parents' first meet-
ing in this heart-warming
and unusual story of families
and family history, which
bridges the gap between
young and old.
☆

DON'T LOOK BEHIND YOU
Lois Duncan
Puffin pbk £4.25
ISBN 0140372938

A gripping and immensely
readable thriller in which
April Corrigan attempts
to recover her lost identity
with dramatic and powerful
results.

ZLATA'S DIARY
Zlata Filipovic
Puffin pbk £3.99
ISBN 0140374639

The diary of 13 year-old Zlata is, perhaps, the most moving account of the war in former Yugoslavia. In it she describes the changes to her home in Sarajevo in 1992. As harrowing as Anne Frank's diary, this account at least ends in escape to Paris for Zlata.

MADAME DOUBTFIRE
Anne Fine
Puffin pbk £4.50
ISBN 0140373551

Madame Doubtfire is the cleaning lady with a lot more up her sleeve as the Hillard family discover! A black comedy telling of the absurdities of divorce.

THE DIARY OF ANNE FRANK
Pan pbk £3.99
ISBN 0330308300

The famous diary of a young girl in war-torn Amsterdam, who heroically saves lives in her cramped attic. Entries of childlike spontaneity are mixed with passages of startling maturity, reflection, optimism and wit.

Rosa Guy

Rosa Guy's books deal with issues faced by young blacks in Harlem, using her own experiences to create a compassionate and uncompromising style.

THE FRIENDS
ISBN 0140366164

EDITH JACKSON
ISBN 0140373020
Puffin pbk £4.50

'The Friends' is a moving story of friendship, trust and betrayal between two young girls in Harlem, facing abuse, hostility and poverty. 'Edith Jackson' continues with the growing awareness of Edith as a young black woman.

WHEN YOU CAN'T SAY NO
Sylvia Hall
Scholastic pbk £5.99
ISBN 059055669X

An eloquent portrayal of the torment, confusion and desperation caused by sexual abuse, not only for the victim, but for all those close to her. It shows sensitively that through the pain and despair can come hope.

QUANTOCK QUARTET
Ruth Elwin Harris
Walker pbk £3.99 each

THE SILENT SHORE

THE BECKONING HILLS

THE DIVIDING SEA

BEYOND THE ORCHID HOUSE

The vivid and memorable saga of the lives and loves of four sisters, each told in a different book, with each reflecting on the others. A moving, compelling chronicle of family life in the first half of the twentieth century.

THE FROZEN WATERFALL
Gaye Hicyilmaz
Faber pbk £3.99
ISBN 0571171613

A novel charting a hunger for knowledge which is invaded by political circumstance. Unusual, often moving, it reflects at length upon the fight for personal freedom during a Turkish family's move to Switzerland.

BUDDY
Nigel Hinton
Puffin pbk £3.99
ISBN 0140371761

Buddy's life is in a state of turmoil; his mum has left, his dad is turning to crime and who, or what is the Beast? A fast moving and down-to-earth story of growing up.

THE OUTSIDERS
S E Hinton
Collins pbk £3.99
ISBN 0006722253

A rites of passage novel of gang life and academic ambition. Often violent but always entertaining, it raises questions about justice, prejudice and the way people respond to poverty. Written when Hinton was herself a teenager in the 60's, it has become a cult classic.

RUMBLEFISH
S E Hinton
Collins pbk £3.50
ISBN 0006712100X

Rusty James wants to be like his older brother, the

Motorcycle Boy, ex-gang leader and respected by all. But his ambition and desire lead to an intense and poignant ending. An exploration of belonging and growing up.

MAPHEAD
Lesley Howarth
Walker pbk £3.99
ISBN 0744536472
The need to belong is explored powerfully in this original novel of Boothe and Powers (visitors from the subtle world) and their gypsy existence on earth. Strange and compelling.

☆

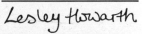

Lesley wrote a thesis on horror movies at college and, before becoming a writer, had numerous jobs (some of them horrible) such as market gardener, flower picker, nursing auxiliary and cook. She now lives in Cornwall and writes full-time, quite happily.

CHILDREN OF THE DUST
Louise Lawrence
Red Fox pbk £3.50
ISBN 0099314118

Surviving nuclear war begs the question 'Would it have been better to have perished?' But no one could have predicted what survivors would live to see. A dark tale for the nuclear age.

THE TWELFTH DAY OF JULY
Joan Lingard
Puffin pbk £3.99
ISBN 0140371753

The first in the Kevin and Sadie Belfast tales. One night Kevin and his Catholic friends sneak into 'Protestant country' and deface a mural, enraging Sadie and her friends. This starts off a series of incidents which culminate in tragedy on the 12th July.

ACROSS THE BARRICADES
Joan Lingard
Puffin pbk £4.50
ISBN 0140371796

Kevin and Sadie know they are in an impossible situation. He is Catholic and she is Protestant and in Belfast friendships between the two groups are taboo. Can love really conquer all?

THE GIVER
Lois Lowry
Collins pbk £3.50
ISBN 0006748287

Trapped in a conformist society, Jon uncovers dark secrets which lead him to undertake an incredible journey. A bold and imaginative tale of one boy's struggle for independence and freedom.

Michelle Magorian

Author of the classic 'Goodnight Mr Tom', she manages to bring together memorable characters, unusual storylines and historical settings to create lasting novels.

A LITTLE LOVE SONG
Michelle Magorian
Mammoth pbk £3.99
ISBN 0749410616

It is 1943 and, evacuated to a sleepy seaside town, Rose and Diane are, for the first time, free of adult restrictions. Both girls begin a summer of self-discovery in this touching story of independence and first love.

THE CHANGEOVER
Margaret Mahy
Puffin pbk £4.50
ISBN 0140372954

This many-layered blend of supernatural thriller and romantic novel explores the complexities of family ties and loyalty as Laura goes through her 'changeover' into a witch in order to save her possessed brother, and encounters the mysterious, intense Sorry Carlisle.

FEET AND OTHER STORIES
Jan Mark
Puffin pbk £3.99
ISBN 0140327975

Eight entertainingly witty and poignant short stores which poke fun at teen angst and anguish.

THEY DO THINGS DIFFERENTLY THERE
Jan Mark
Red Fox pbk £3.50
ISBN 0099264218

A group of individual portraits drawn together to form a stunning tale. An inspired account of two teenagers who appear not to fit into the world around them. Yet once you take a closer look at that world, is it any surprise..?

BLAEBERRY SUNDAY
Elizabeth O'Hara
Poolbeg Press pbk £3.99
ISBN 1853713600

Sally is sick of being a hired serving girl and returns home to Glenbra, only to encounter more hardships. Nothing, however, is as overwhelming as her love for Manus, and she waits anxiously to see him on the fateful Blaeberry Sunday. A bittersweet tale set in 1890's Ireland.

TASTING THE THUNDER
Gary Paulsen
Macmillan pbk £3.50
ISBN 0330327054

Running away isn't as easy as it sounds for one sixteen year-old boy who encounters cruelty, hard times and an array of strange characters. Farm and fairground life provide little comfort in this detailed novel. Paulsen has a clipped, original voice.

HATCHET
Gary Paulsen
Macmillan pbk £3.99
ISBN 0330310453

When a small plane crashes in the Canadian wilderness, 13 year-old Brian has to quickly learn how to survive, the hard way. A gripping, heart-stopping story of a boy's fight to survive under extreme circumstances.

UNDER THE BLOOD RED SUN
Graham Salisbury
Scholastic pbk £6.99
ISBN 0590541870

Tomi is a young Japanese American living in Hawaii during WWII. His peaceful life is turned upside down when the Japanese bomb Pearl Harbour and Tomi suddenly finds himself an alien in his own land. With his father and grandfather in an internment camp, Tomi is left to protect his mother and sister in a hostile world.

WHY WEEPS THE BROGAN
Hugh Scott
Walker pbk £3.99
ISBN 0744520401

Saxon and Gilbert live out a ritualised, indoor existence 4 years and 81 days after nuclear hostilities, guarding against the disturbing, weeping Brogan. A compelling and unsettling examination of life after nuclear war.

THE BOY IN THE BUBBLE
Ian Strachan
Mammoth pbk £3.50
ISBN 0749716851

A powerful, heart-warming story about a girl's budding relationship with a boy isolated by his illness. Adam cannot leave the safety of his isolation tent and so Anne becomes his 'life-taster'. This emotionally draining book is as affecting as Adam's illness, and is written with compassion and warmth.

Robert Swindells

Swindells is a well-established author with an enviable history of successful and award-winning books to his name. Stepping into the minds of young people with apparent ease and psychological insight, he never shies away from difficult issues.

STONE COLD
Puffin pbk £3.99
ISBN 0140362517

Link runs away to London to escape his stepfather and ends up living rough on the streets, where he encounters a frightening and dangerous world. A powerful, chilling and disturbingly realistic examination of our attitudes to the homeless.

Gary Paulsen

Gary Paulsen's own life is the stuff of fiction.
He had a difficult childhood and ran away at the age of 14,
travelled with a carnival and drank heavily for many years.
He has raced across Alaska on a dog-sled, been attacked by
a moose, trapped in icy water, sailed the Pacific and been
dragged unconscious by dogs.

When he stopped drinking he became one
of America's most prolific authors for young
people and one of its bestselling, after winning
the prestigious Newbery Award for *Ice Race*
and also for *Hatchet*.

Paulsen got his love for books from a librarian.
'It didn't matter that my clothes were wrong,
that my folks were drunks, that I wasn't
accepted by my peers ... she gave me writing
which I love, she gave me the whole world.'

Paulsen has been described as a Jack London
for teenagers and his books have the same passionate,
adventurous streak.

Some books by Gary Paulsen

Hatchet	**Hatchet: The Return**
The Voyage of the Frog	**Hatchet: Winter**
The Fourteenth Summer	**Harris & Me**
Canyons	*(all published by Macmillan)*

BROTHER IN THE LAND
Puffin pbk £4.50
ISBN 0140373004

A hard-hitting account of a teenage boy's struggle to survive and protect his younger brother after the holocaust. Disturbing and thought provoking.

Mildred D Taylor

Taylor's passionate and emotionally charged series of novels, set in the American deep south in the 1930's and 1940's, follows the lives of Cassie Logan and her family as they struggle against racism, oppression and financial hardships to retain their land, their lives and their dignities.

ROLL OF THUNDER HEAR MY CRY
ISBN 0140371745

LET THE CIRCLE BE UNBROKEN
ISBN 0140372903

ROAD TO MEMPHIS
ISBN 014037356X
all Puffin pbk £4.99

THE SECRET DIARY OF ADRIAN MOLE AGED 13 ³/₄
Sue Townsend
Mammoth pbk £3.99
ISBN 0749700092

Debut appearance of the inimitable and hugely popular Adrian Mole, teen-angst superstar and budding poet.

Mole is the archetype of confused adolescence, burgeoning with hopes and desires and Townsend's acute observations make for both cringing identification and the best kind of laugh-out-loud reading. Two sequels are also available.

PROPER LITTLE NOORYEFF
Jean Ure
Corgi pbk £2.99
ISBN 0552527114

Jamie knows what his friends will think if they find out he's going to dance in a ballet show, whether he's a good dancer or not. But the show must go on … A humorous, acutely observant yet compassionate look at male stereotyping and the uncertainties of adolescence.

ALWAYS SEBASTIAN
Jean Ure
Red Fox pbk £3.50
ISBN 0099301989

Sebastian is tall, dark, handsome and is passionate about animal rights. Martha and Sophie like him and have to convince their Mum that he's not dangerous, which is difficult when a bomb has just gone off outside the laboratory …

HOMECOMING
Cynthia Voigt
Collins pbk £3.99
ISBN 0006724590

Dicey and her 3 brothers and sisters are abandoned by their mother in a shopping mall. They are scared and confused but certain of one thing – they must stay together at all costs. Under the strong leadership of Dicey, they undertake a dangerous and epic journey across America in search of an aunt they have never met.

DICEY'S SONG
Cynthia Voigt
Collins pbk £3.99
ISBN 000672566X

The second book in the popular Tillerman saga. Dicey and her brothers and sisters have finally found somewhere they can call home. But life with their Grandmother brings its own problems.

THE SCARECROWS
Robert Westall
Puffin pbk £4.50
ISBN 014037308X

Simon's fury at spending the summer at his hated stepfather's house raises a spirit of powerful enmity-which threatens to consume both him and his family. Only by confronting his own hatred can he lay it to rest and accept the past and the future in this eerie supernatural thriller.

FALLING INTO GLORY
Robert Westall
Mammoth pbk £4.99
ISBN 0749717556

A romp through love and rugby in a Northern school during the 1950's. Westall treats the subject of love between pupil and teacher with a wry sensitivity and sometimes uncomfortable realism.

FALLING APART
Jacqueline Wilson
Collins pbk £3.99
ISBN 0006740537

Girl meets boy and falls in love. But Tina is 15 and goes to Bridge Street Comprehensive, and Simon is a sixth former at an exclusive public school. A gripping and moving novel exploring the intensity and longing of first love and the devastating impact of bereavement and loss.

THE PIGMAN
Paul Zindel
Red Fox pbk £3.50
ISBN 0099184311

Two teenagers befriend a lonely old man – the Pigman – but their mindless misuse of his kindness has tragic results. Zindel's classic novel of teenage disorientation and disillusionment is fast-paced, witty and moving.

Teenage Health

HAVE YOU STARTED YET?
Ruth Thomson
Macmillan pbk £3.99
ISBN 033033722X

A friendly and straightforward guide to all aspects of menstruation. This illustrated book successfully tackles all the questions raised during a time of increasing self-awareness and personal change.

THE DIARY OF A TEENAGE HEALTH FREAK
Aidan MacFarlane and Ann MacPherson
Oxford pbk £3.50
ISBN 0192860836

Hilariously funny diaries of Peter Payne, 14 year old confirmed health freak and hypochondriac, covering subjects as diverse as acne, warts, alcohol, drugs, headaches, sex and a host of other ailments and illnesses. Written by two practising doctors, this wickedly funny book provides practical information in an easily digestible format.

THIRTEEN SOMETHING
Jane Goldman
Puffin pbk £3.99
ISBN 0140371958

A successful attempt to tackle every aspect of this difficult time for adolescents. Goldman covers a range of subjects, including friends, food, leisure and clothes. She looks at issues from both a male and female point of view.

For more books on puberty - see the health section in Reference.

Did you Know?

Paul Zindel was born in New York. When he was 15 he contracted TB and had to spend 18 months in a sanatorium. This made him miss graduating with his class but it did give him lots of ideas that he used later in his books.

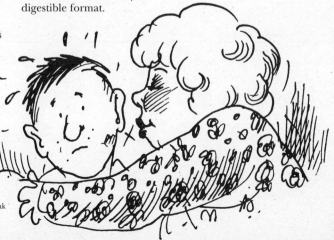

The Diary of a Teenage Health Freak

Teenage Series

Series, such as Point Horror and Sweet Valley High are incredibly popular with teenagers and continue to be produced and read on a mass scale. As a parent or teacher, (or bookseller!) it can be frustrating to watch these formulaic titles being devoured, and yet in some ways, any reading is good reading. There are so many other distractions at this age that maintaining a reading habit at all can be a major achievement. Take advantage of their enthusiasm and use our guide to introduce them to some more challenging authors.

POINT SERIES
Published by Scholastic

'Point' has become the overall name for what is really an industry of generic fiction, ranging from crime and science fiction to the phenomenally successful Point Horror series. American in origin and using different authors (look out for good ones like Diane Hor), Point play at being adult books (gilt lettering, screaming covers) but are actually fairly safe reads.
There has been a lot of controversy around horror for children and although Point Horror books are suspenseful and creepy, the gore-factor is pretty low (unlike some of their less credible imitators) and they

are actually very moral in tone with good generally winning out over evil.

MAKING OUT SERIES
Katherine Applegate
Macmillan pbk £2.99 each

The copyline is 'The new series about falling in love' and the titles are 'Zoey fools Around', 'Jake Finds Out' etc. The book jackets could be covers of a teenage magazine – they are fashionable and stylish, making their competitors look old-hat. Based on a group of eight friends on a small island and their romantic escapades, this is good escapist fiction for wannabe 17 year olds.

What to read now

The move from the safety of the children's book to the enormous and sometimes intimidating adult book world can be difficult for even the most confident readers. Here are some good books and authors to start with:

GENERAL FICTION

The Catcher in the Rye
by JD Salinger

To Kill a Mockingbird
by Harper Lee

Oranges are Not The Only Fruit *by Jeanette Winterson*

The Dark Quartet
by Lynne Reid Banks

The Buddha of Suburbia
by Hanif Kureishi

Fatherland
by Robert Harris

The Color Purple
by Alice Walker

Cold Comfort Farm
by Stella Gibbons

On the Road
by Jack Kerouac

Ben Elton

Roddy Doyle

Daphne Du Maurier

CRIME FICTION

Ruth Rendell

Colin Dexter

Raymond Chandler

SCIENCE FICTION

Tom Holt

Iain Banks

Douglas Adams

Terry Pratchett

Robert Rankin

BIOGRAPHY

Jung Chang

Laurie Lee

Roald Dahl

Karen Blixen

POETRY

Simon Armitage

Wendy Cope

Carol Ann Duffy

John Hegley

Have you heard about 'In Brief'?

In Brief began as a local initiative in Newcastle when Elizabeth Hammill of Waterstone's began working with local teenagers to review books. It is now a nationally distributed magazine, produced three times a year and read by teenagers, teachers, parents and librarians.

Anne Fine, Robert Cormier, Francine Pascal and William Mayne are among the authors who have been interviewed, and there are regular pieces on prizes, publishing trends and other book related issues. The magazine is free from outside influence, full of fresh ideas and occasionally controversial. "In my mind In Brief has now jumped from 'a jolly good thing' to 'required reading for all authors'" Robert Westall (Author)

"I enjoy reading as the reviews are totally candid and honest – you know the reviewer isn't doing a favour to a friend... I think the open forum for discussions with authors and editors is excellent, and probably unique" Linda Newbury (Author and School Librarian)

HOW CAN YOU GET IN BRIEF?

In Brief is available for free in all branches of Waterstone's at the time of publication. For your convenience you can subscribe to the magazine by filling out the form below.

Services at Waterstone's
RECOMMENDATION

Our booksellers really know and care about what they are selling. If you need help, please don't hesitate to ask.

WRITERS AT WATERSTONE'S

Ask at your branch for details of author events (including children's events).

WATERSTONE'S MAILING SERVICE

Waterstone's mail order facility: Waterstone's Mailing Service, 4-5 Milsom Street, Bath BA1 1DA

BOOKSEARCH

Waterstone's Booksearch service will try to track down out-of-print books for you. Booksearch, 32-40 Calverley Road, Tunbridge Wells, TN1 2TD

SIGNED FIRST EDITIONS

A choice of up to 150 of the year's finest fiction and non-fiction titles – all signed by the author and posted to you. Waterstone's Signed First Editions Collection, 4-5 Milsom Street, Bath BA1 1DA

WATERSTONE'S BOOK VOUCHERS

Accepted in over 500 book-shops in the United Kingdom and Ireland, including all branches of W H Smith.

For information about any Waterstone's service, please ask a bookseller.

I would like to receive the next three issues of *In Brief*...

Please send them to me at:

Name

Address

Postcode

I enclose a cheque for £6.00, made payable to Waterstone's Booksellers, to cover my subscription.

Send your subscription form to this address:

In Brief... Subscriptions
Waterstone's
Capital Court
Capital Interchange Way
Brentford
TW8 0EX

W

Subject index

Here are some suggestions for books and authors which might help you with special interests or needs.

ABUSE
Break in the Sun
Melusine
When You Can't Say No

ADOPTION & FOSTERING
Anne of Green Gables
Back Home
Ballet Shoes
Dicey's Song
Down Came a Blackbird
Edith Jackson
Goodnight Mr Tom
Great Elephant Chase
Monkey Island
The Demon Headmaster
The Story of Tracey Beaker
The Trouble with Donovan Croft

ADVENTURE (SEE ALSO THRILLERS)
Asterix
Gary Paulsen
Hiding Out
Jackson & Livingstone books
Low Tide
Memoirs of a Dangerous Alien
Saga of Erik the Viking
Swallows and Amazons
The Great Elephant Chase
Tintin
Willard Price Books

ANGER
George's Marvellous Medicine
Goggle Eyes
Matilda
The Magic Finger

ANIMALS
Animals of Farthing Wood
Beatrix Potter
Brian Jacques
Dick King-Smith
Dr Xargle
Hairy McLary
How Dogs Really Work
Lucy Daniels
Rudyard Kipling
Tarka the Otter
The Incredible Journey
The Whale's Song
The Wind in the Willows
Watership Down
Willard Price

BABIES
Dr Xargle
Janine & the New Baby
Mummy Laid an Egg
Peepo

BALLET STORIES
Ballet Shoes
Orchard Book of Stories from the Ballet
Scrambled Legs

BULLYING
Blubber
Bully (Coppard)
Bully (Hughes)
Eighteenth Emergency
Farmer Duck
Krindlekrax
Listen to the Dark
Matilda
The Diddakoi
Willy the Wimp

COMPUTERS & TECHNOLOGY
The Computer Nut
Hacker

DEATH & BEREAVEMENT
Badger's Parting Gifts
Bridge to Terabithia
Charlotte's Web
Double Image
Falling Apart
Goodnight Mr Tom
Granpa
Parcel of Patterns
See Ya Simon
The Diddakoi
The Secret Garden
The Spying Game
Tiger Eyes
Two Weeks with the Queen
Walkabout

DIVORCE & SINGLE PARENT FAMILIES
Buddy
Divorce Express
Goggle Eyes
Henry's Leg
Josie Smith
Madame Doubtfire
The Man Whose Mother Was a Pirate
The Suitcase Kid

EATING PROBLEMS & DISORDERS
Oliver's Vegetables
Eat up Gemma
Blubber

ENVIRONMENTAL ISSUES
Rainforest
Dinosaurs & all that Rubbish
Window

Oi, Get off our Train
Dear Greenpeace
The Magic Finger
The Iron Man
The Iron Woman
Earth to Matthew
Run with the Wind
Why the Whales Came
Brother Eagle, Sister Sky

FANTASY
Alice in Wonderland
Beaver Towers
Box of Delights
Dark is Rising
Finn Family Moonintroll
Moondial
Narnia series
Peter Pan
Philip Ridley Books
Steps up the Chimney
Sword in the Stone
The Borrowers
The Changeover
The Haunting
The Lives of Christopher Chant
The Magic Finger
The Weirdstone of Brisingamen
Wizard of Earthsea

FEAR (SEE PHOBIAS)

FUNNY STORIES
David Henry Wilson
Flat Stanley
Jacqueline Wilson
Kingfisher book of Funny Stories
Krindlekrax
Maurice Gleitzman
Paul Jennings
Paula Danziger
Roald Dahl
Scrambled Legs
The Phantom Tollbooth

GENDER ISSUES
Bill's New Frock
Diary of a Teenage Health Freak
Flour Babies
Handles
Happy Families
Karate Princess
Mildred D Taylor
Ms Wiz
Paper Bag Princess
Pippi Longstocking
Princess Smartypants
Willy the Wimp

GHOSTS (SEE ALSO THRILLERS)
Down Came a Blackbird
The Haunting
The Scarecrows

HISTORICAL PERIODS
(SEE ALSO WAR)

PREHISTORY
Stig of the Dump
Sun Horse Moon Horse
VIKINGS & ROMANS
Asterix
Eagle of the Ninth
The Saga of Eric the Viking

TUDORS & STUARTS
Parcel of Patterns
The Wool Pack
Traveller in Time

VICTORIANS
Street Child
The Secret Garden
Tom's Midnight Garden

EARLY 20TH CENTURY
Charlotte Sometimes
Mildred D Taylor
Pigeon Summer
The Family from One End Street
The Secret Garden
Wreck of the Zanzibar

ILLNESS & DISABILITY
Blabber Mouth
Bully (Coppard)
Heidi
Listen to the Dark
See Ya Simon
The Boy in the Bubble
The Cay
The Secret Garden
Two Weeks with the Queen

INTERACTIVE TITLES
Castle of Fear
Jackson & Livingstone
Pop Up Books
Puzzle Adventures
Very Hungry Caterpillar
Where's Wally
Fantastic Maze Book

IRISH INTEREST
Blaeberry Sunday
Circling the Triangle
Joan Lingard
Real Cool
Run with the Wind
Under the Hawthorn Tree

JEALOUSY
Bel Mooney
Goggle Eyes
Titch

LONELINESS & FRIENDSHIP
Amber Brown is not a Crayon
BFG
Charlotte's Web
Listen to the Dark
Moondial
My Best Friend
One More River
The Friends
Winnie the Witch

MOVING HOME
Amber Brown is not a Crayon
Back Home
Paper Faces
Starring Sally J Freeman as Herself
Superfudge
The Bed & Breakfast Star
The Peppermint Pig
The Suitcase Kid
Thunder & Lightnings

MULTI-CULTURAL BOOKS
A Carribean Dozen
Amazing Grace
Brother Eagle, Sister Sky
Diddakoi
Eat up Gemma
Hurricane Betsy
I am David
Jamaica's Find
Janine & the New Baby
Julian Stories
Mildred D Taylor
Rosa Guy
Talking Turkeys
The Patchwork Quilt
The Trouble with Donovan Croft
Walkabout

MYSTERY STORIES
Melusine
Mystery Club
Sam the Girl Detective

PONY STORIES
Black Beauty
Jinny Stories
The Enchanted Horse

PHOBIAS
GENERAL -
Otherwise Known as Sheila the Great

DARK
The Bear under the Stairs
Owl who was Afraid of the Dark
SLEEP
Can't You Sleep Little Bear

RACISM ISSUES
Iggie's House
Mildred D Taylor
Rosa Guy
My Mate Shofiq

RELUCTANT READERS
(see interactive titles)
Anastasia
Asterix
Don Quixote
Enid Blyton
Rudley Cabot
Soccer at Sandford
Sweet Valley series
The babysitters club
The Fib
The Great Smile Robbery
Tintin

ROMANCE
A Little Love Song
Boy in the Bubble
Circling the Triangle
Falling into Glory
Forever
Gregory's Girl
Making Out series
Sweet Valley High

SCHOOL STORIES
Dragon in Class 4
Goalkeepers Revenge
Mr Majeika
Ms Wiz
My Teacher is an Alien
Please Mrs Butler
School
The Demon Headmaster
The Fib
The School at the Chalet series
The Turbulent Term of Tyke Tiler
The Worst Witch
Trebizon books

SCIENCE & TECHNOLOGY
Russell Stannard's books

SCIENCE FICTION
Rebecca's World
Tripods Trilogy
My Teacher is an Alien
Memoirs of a Dangerous Alien

SCOTTISH INTEREST
Jinny stories
Josie Smith
Katie Morag & the Two
Grandmothers
Scottish Folk Tales

SEX & SEXUALITY
Are you there God,
It's me, Margaret
Dance on My Grave
Dear Nobody
Forever
Mummy Laid an Egg
The Pigman
When You Can't Say No

SIBLING RIVALRY
Fudge-a-mania
Horrid Henry
The Stone Mouse

SPORTS
Gregory's Girl
Napper
Soccer at Sandford
The Big series

THRILLERS & SCARY STORIES
A Creepy Company
Goosebumps
Lois Duncan
Oxford Book of Scary Tales
RL Stine
Robert Cormier
Room 13
Scare yourself to Sleep
The Haunting of Cassie Palmer
Treasury of Spooky Stories
Whispers in the Graveyard

TRAVEL - IMAGINARY & TIME TRAVEL
Around the World in 80 Days
Charlotte Sometimes
Moondial
Tom's Midnight Garden
Traveller in Time
Where's Julius

WAR & CONFLICT
Back Home
Brother in the Land
Changes Trilogy
Children of the Dust
Chocolate War
Joan Lingard
One More River
The Frozen Waterfull
The Outsiders
Z for Zachariah
Zlata's Diary

WIZARDS & WITCHES
Carbonel
Meg & Mog
Mr Majeika
Ms Wiz
Simon & the Witch
The Witches
The Wizard of Oz
The Worst Witch

WORLD WAR II
Carrie's War
Conrad's War
Diary of Anne Frank
Going Solo
In Time of War
Michelle Magorian
Paper Faces
Robert Westall
Starring Sally J Freeman
as Herself
The Silver Sword
War Boy
When Hitler Stole
Pink Rabbit

FURTHER RESOURCES

If you wish to seek out more in-depth help for your child's needs, then these Associations may be able to help:

Young Book Trust
Tel: 0181 870 9055

Young Book Trust Scotland
Tel: 0131 229 3663
(for special needs booklists, author information and general advice)

National Library for the Handicapped Child
Tel: 01734 891101
(books in braille, large print, signed language, videos of books)

100 Multi Cultural Picture Books Working Group against Racism in Children's Resources
Tel: 0171 627 4594

Welsh Book Council
Tel: 01970 624151

Children's Literature Association of Ireland
Church of Ireland College of Education
96 Upper Rathmines Road
Dublin 6

British Dyslexia Association
98 London Road
Reading RG1 5AU

The Poetry Library
Tel: 0171 921 0664

Jolly Roger

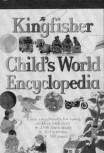
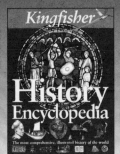

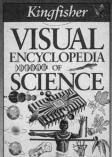

AWARD WINNING CHILDREN'S BOOKS

There are scores of medals awarded for outstanding children's books every year. They range from environmental awards to awards from magazines to awards with winners chosen by children. We have listed some of the more prestigious prizes and their recent winners below:

CARNEGIE MEDAL

This award was established in 1936 and is awarded to an outstanding book for children written in English. Early winners included Noel Streatfield, CS Lewis, Alan Garner and Arthur Ransome. In recent years the prize has received controversial coverage for its choice of hard-hitting winners.

1985   Storm
        Kevin Crossley-Holland

1986   Granny was a Buffer Girl
        Berlie Doherty

1987   The Ghost Drum
        Susan Price

1988   A Pack of Lies
        Geraldine McCaughrean

1989   Goggle Eyes
        Anne Fine

1990   Wolf
        Gillian Cross

1991   Dear Nobody
        Berlie Doherty

1992   Flour Babies
        Anne Fine

1993   Stone Cold
        Robert Swindells

1994   Whispers in the Graveyard
        Theresa Breslin

KATE GREENAWAY MEDAL

Established in 1955, this prize is awarded to a children's book illustrator for a work published in the UK. Early winners read like a who's who of 20th century children's illustrations with such names as Edward Ardizzone, Brian Wildsmith, Raymond Briggs, Shirley Hughes and Helen Oxenbury.

1985   Sir Gawain & the
        Loathly Lady
        Juan Wijngaard

1986   Snow White in New York
        Fiona French

1987   Crafty Chameleon
        Adrienne Kennaway

1988   Can't You Sleep Little Bear
        Barbara Firth

1989   War Boy
        Michael Foreman

1990   The Whale's Song
        Gary Blythe

1991   The Jolly Christmas
        Postman
        Janet & Allan Ahlberg

1992   Zoo
        Anthony Browne

1993   Black Ships Before Troy
        Alan Lee

1994   Way Home
        Gregory Rogers

GUARDIAN CHILDREN'S FICTION AWARD

Established in 1967 and awarded to an outstanding work of fiction for children written by a British or Commonwealth author. Early winners were Joan Aiken, Nina Bawdsen and Peter Dickinson.

1985   What is Truth
        Ted Hughes

1986   Henry's Leg
        Ann Pilling

1987   The True Story of Spit McPhee
        James Aldridge

1988   The Runaways
        Ruth Thomas

1989   A Pack of Lies
        Geraldine McCaughrean

1990   Goggle Eyes
        Anne Fine

1991   The Kingdom by the Sea
        Robert Westall

1992   Paper Faces
        Rachel Anderson

        The Exiles
        Hilary McKay

1993   Low Tide
        William Mayne

1994   The Mennyms
        Sylvia Waugh

1995   Maphead
        Lesley Howarth

WATERSTONE'S CHILDREN'S BOOKS OF THE MONTH

A monthly award chosen by booksellers throughout the company, this has come to represent the very best of what is new in children's books.

1995

January
The Bed & Breakfast Star
Jacqueline Wilson

February
Uncle Albert & the
Quantum Quest
Russell Stannard

March
Operation Gadgetman
Malorie Blackman

April
Stone Cold
Robert Swindells

May
Pirate (Eyewitness)
Richard Platt

June
Cruel Kings & Mean Queens
Terry Deary

July
Where's Wally in Hollywood
Martin Handford

August
Oliver's Vegetables
French & Bartlett

September
The Last Noo Noo
Jill Murphy

October
The Treasury of Children's
Literature
Alison Sage (ed.)

November
Maisy's House
Lucy Cousins

December
Maths Curse
Scieska & Smith

Index

AUTHOR AND TITLE INDEX

101 Dalmations **81**
Across The Barricades **109**
Adams, Richard **51**
Adrian Mole **112**
Aesop's Fables **45**
After the First Death **106**
Agard, John **92,93**
Ahlberg, Allan **33,51,93**
Ahlberg, Janet & Allan **9,12,35**
Aiken, Joan **51,105**
AK **107**
Alborough, Jez **12**
Alcock, Vivien **51**
Alcott, Louisa May **51**
Alderson, Brian **47**
Alfie's Feet **19**
Alice in Wonderland **57**
All in One Piece **22**
Allan, Tony **47**
Always Sebastian **112**
Alphabugs **10**
Amery, Heather **8,15**
Amazing Grace **32**
Amber Brown is Not a Crayon **37**
Anancy & Mr Drybone **48**
Anastasia Krupnik **72**
Andersen, Hans Christian **45**
Anderson, Rachel **51**
Animals of Farthing Wood **60**
Anne of Green Gables **75**
Applegate, Katherine **114**
Arabian Nights **47**
Arctic Adventure **78**
Are You There God? It's Me,
Margaret **53**
Arkle, Phyllis **35**
Armitage, David & Rhonda **12**
Around the World in 80 Days **83**
Ashley, Bernard **52**
Asquith, Ros **105**
Asterix **64**
Awdrey, Rev. **12**
Babysitters Club **73**
Back Home **72**
Badger's Parting Gifts **26**
Ballet Shoes **82**
Banks, Lynne Reid **52,105**
Barber, Antonia **12**
Barrie, JM **52**
Barry, Margaret Stuart **35**
Bartlett, Alison **18**
Baum, Frank L **52**
Bawden, Nina **52**
Bayley, Nicola **12**
Bear under the Stairs **16**
Beaver Towers **66**
Beck, Ian **9,13,46**

Bed & Breakfast Star **86**
Beginner Books **33**
Belloc, Hilaire **93**
Benson, Gerald **92**
Best Friends **77**
Beware of Boys **13**
BFG **58**
Bible **102**
Biesty, Stephe **102**
Big...series **37**
Bill's New Frock **38**
Blabber Mouth **64**
Black Beauty **79**
Black Ships Before Troy **48**
Blacker, Terence **34,35**
Blackman, Malorie **35,52**
Blaeberry Sunday **110**
Blake, Quentin **13,31,92**
Blessu **39**
Blitzcat **85**
Blubber **53**
Blume, Judy **35,53,105**
Blundell, Tony **13**
Blythe, Gary **25**
Blyton, Enid **53**
Bond, Michael **35**
Book of 20th Century Verse **89**
Book of Children's Poetry **91**
Book of Comic Verse **91**
Book of Mythology **47**
Book of Nonsense Verse **92**
Borrowers **77**
Boston, Lucy M **55**
Box of Delights **75**
Boy in the Bubble **110**
Boy & Going Solo **58**
Bradman, Tony **35,36**
Brent Dyer, Elinor M **55**
Breslin, Theresa **55**
Brierley, Louise **48**
Bridge to Terabithia **77**
Briggs, Raymond **13,31,56**
Brisley, Joyce Lankester **36**
Brother Eagle, Sister Sky **31**
Brother in the Land **112**
Browne, Anthony **13**
Brown, Jeff **36**
Brown, Ruth **12,13**
Brumpton, Keith **56**
Bruna, Dick **14**
Buddy **108**
Bully (David Hughes) **32**
Bully (Yvonne Coppard) **57**
Burnett, Frances H **56**
Burnford, Sheila **56**
Burningham, John **14**
Burstyn, Patrick **56**
But Where is The Green Parrot **27**
Butterworth, Nick **14,21**
Byars, Betsy **56**
Cameron, Ann **36**

Campbell, Rod **14,17**
Can't You Sleep Little Bear **26**
Carbonel **79**
Caribbean Dozen **92**
Carle, Eric **15**
Carpenter, Humphrey **36,79**
Carrie's War **52**
Carroll, Lewis **57**
Carter, David **10**
Castle of Fear **56**
Cartwright, Stephen **8,15**
Cat Ate My Gymsuit **107**
Cautionary Verses **93**
Cay, The **83**
Chamberlain, Margaret **22**
Chambers, Aidan **105**
Changeover **109**
Changes Trilogy **107**
Charlie & the Chocolate
Factory **58**
Charlotte Sometimes **61**
Charlotte's Web **85**
Chief Seattle **31**
Children of Green Knowe **55**
Children of the Dust **109**
Child's Book of Art **99**
Childs, Rob **37,57**
Chocolate War **106**
Chocolate Wedding **32**
Christopher, John **57**
Circling the Triangle **107**
Civardi, Anne **8**
Clarke, Vanessa **9**
Cleary, Beverly **57**
Clever Polly & the
Stupid Wolf **42**
Clocks & More Clocks **19**
Cole, Babette **15,31**
Cole, Gerald **106**
Computer Nut **56**
Conlon-McKenna, Marita **57**
Conrad's War **60**
Coolidge, Susan **57**
Cooper, Helen **16**
Cooper, Susan **57**
Coppard, Yvonne **57,106**
Corbett, Pie **9**
Corlett, William **57**
Cormier, Robert **106**
Counsel, June **37**
Cousins, Lucy **10,11,16**
Coville, Bruce **58**
Cowcher, Helen **16**
Creation Stories **48**
Creepy Company **105**
Cresswell, Helen **37,58**
Cross, Gillian **58**
Crowther, Robert **10**
Cruickshank, Margaret **107**

Curry, Jennifer **91,92**
Dahl, Roald **31,37,58,94**
Dalton, Annie **59**
Dance on My Grave **105**
Dancing Bear **40**
Daniels, Lucy **60**
Danny, Champion of the World **59**
Dann, Colin **60**
Danziger, Paula **37,60,107**
Dark Dark Tale **13**
Dark is Rising Sequence **57**
Davies, Andrew **60,61**
Day Jake Vacuumed **20**
Day the Smells Went Wrong **42**
Dear Greenpeace **20**
Dear Nobody **107**
Dear Zoo **14**
Deary, Terry **101, 100**
Demon Headmaster **58**
Diary of a Teenage Health Freak **113**
Diary of Anne Frank **108**
Dicey's Song **112**
Dictionaries **99,100**
Dickinson, Peter **107**
Diddakoi **65**
Digby, Anne **61**
Dilly the Dinosaur **35**
Dinosaurs & All That Rubbish.**16**
Dirty Beasts **94**
Divorce Express **107**
Doctor Dolittle **72**
Dodd, Lynley **16**
Dogger **19**
Doherty, Berlie **61,107**
Don Quixote **33**
Don't Do That **24**
Don't Look Behind You **107**
Double Image **75**
Down Came a Blackbird **85**
Dr Xargle's Book of Eartlets **27**
Dracula's Castle **82**
Dragon in Class 4 **37**
Duffy, Carol Ann **93**
Duncan, Lois **107**
Each Peach, Pear, Plum **12**
Eagle of the Ninth **82**
Earth to Matthew **60**
Eat Up Gemma **18**
Eccleshare, Julia **89**
Edith Jackson **108**
Educating Marmalade **61**
Edwards, Dorothy **37**
Ehrlich, Amy **46**
Eighteenth Emergency **56**
Elboz, Stephen **61**
Elephant and Bad Baby **26**
Elmer **7,22**
Emil and the Detectives **70**
Enchanted Horse **41**
Enchanted Wood **53**
Encyclopedias **99**

English Folktales **45**
Enormous Crocodile **31**
Eva **107**
Everybody Else Does, Why Can't I **106**
Exiles, The **75**
Eyewitness Atlas of World **99**
Eyewitness Series **99**
Fairy Tales **45,46**
Falling Apart **113**
Falling into Glory **113**
Family from One End Street **62**
Fancy That **10**
Fantastic Maze Book **81**
Fantastic Mr Fox **37**
Farmer Duck **26**
Farmer, Penelope **61**
Farmyard Tales Series **15**
Falkner, JM **61**
Favourite Tales **33**
Feet & Other Stories **109**
Fib& Other Stories **72**
Filipovic, Zlata **108**
Fine, Anne **38,62,108**
Finn Family Moomintroll **68**
First 1000 Words **8**
First Discovery Series **99**
First Experiences **8**
First Fairy Tales **46**
First Focus Baby Books **7**
First Poems **89**
First Term at Trebizon **61**
First Young Puffin Book
of Bedtime Stories **39**
Firth, Barbara **26**
Fisk, Pauline **62**
Fitzhugh, Louise **62**
Five Children & It **76**
Flat Stanley **36**
Flour Babies **62**
Flournoy, Val **31**
Follow that Bus **38**
For the Love of a Horse **72**
Foreman, Michael **9,16,47,62,46**
Forever **105**
Foster, John **89,90,92**
Fowler, Richard **10,16**
Fox, Paula **62**
Frank, Anne **108**
Freckle Juice **35**
French, Fiona **48**
French, Vivian **18**
Friends, The **108**
Frozen Waterfall **108**
Fry, Plantaganet Somerset **100**
Funny Stories **86**
Garfield, Leon **79**
Gargling with Jelly **96**
Garland, Sarah **8**
Garner, Alan **62**
Garnett, Eve **62**
Getting Rich with Jeremy James **86**

Ghost of Thomas Kempe **72**
Gift from Winklesea **37**
Giraffe, The Pelly, and Me **31**
Giver, The **109**
Gleitzman, Morris **64**
Goalkeeper's Revenge **76**
Gobbolino the Witch's Cat **42**
Godden, Rumer **65**
Goggle Eyes **62**
Going to Playschool **8**
Goldman, Jane **113**
Goodnight Mr Tom **73**
Goscinny **64**
Goudge, Elizabeth **65**
Grahame, Kenneth **65**
Granny was a Buffer Girl **107**
Granpa **14**
Great Elephant Chase **58**
Great Smile Robbery **75**
Greek and Norse Legends **48**
Greek Myths for Young Children **47**
Greek Myths, Orchard Book of **48**
Green, Lancelyn Roger **47**
Gregory's Girl **106**
Grimm, Brothers **45**
Grizzly Tales for
Gruesome Kids **78**
Groosham Grange **66**
Guin, Ursula le **65**
Guy, Rosa **108**
Hacker **52**
Hairy MacLary **16**
Hall, Sylvia **108**
Hall, Willis **65**
Handford, Martin **65**
Handles **73**
Happy Families **33**
Harnett, Cynthia **65**
Harriet the Spy **62**
Harris, Ruth Elwin **108**
Harvey, Anne **93**
Hatchet **110**
Haunted House **10**
Haunting of Cassie Palmer **51**
Haunting, The **73**
Have You Started Yet **113**
Havill, Juanita **18**
Hawkins, Colin & Jacqui **31,66**
Hayes, Sarah **18**
Heard it in the Playground **93**
Hedderwick, Mairi **18**
Heide, Florence Parry **38**
Heidi **81**
Henry's Leg **77**
Henry, Maeve **66**
Here Comes Charlie Moon **38**
Herge **66**
Hicyilmaz, Gaye **108**
Hiding Out **71**
Hill, David **66**
Hill, Eric **18**

Hinton, Nigel **66,108**
Hinton, SE **108**
Hissey, Jane **18**
History of Britain & Ireland **100**
History of the World **100**
Hoban, Russell **66**
Hoffman, Mary **32**
Holm, Anne **66**
Homecoming **112**
Hooper, Mary **38**
Horowitz, Anthony **66**
Horrible Histories **100**
Horrid Henry **42**
Hot Dog & Other Poems **96**
House of Rats **61**
House that Sailed Away **38**
How Do I Put it On **9**
How Dogs Really Work **32**
How Your Body Works **102**
Howarth, Lesley **109**
Hughes, David **32**
Hughes, Shirley **8,19,38**
Hughes, Ted **67**
Hurricane Betsy **35**
Hutchinson Treasury of
Children's Literature **86**
Hypnotiser, The **96**
Hutchins, Pat **19,38**
I am David **66**
I am the Cheese **106**
I Can Read **33**
I Din Do Nuttin **93**
I Don't Want To! **40**
I Like this Poem **91**
I Want My Potty **8**
I Want to Be **24**
I Was a Teenage Worrier **105**
I Wouldn't Thank You For A
Valentine **93**
Ibbotson, Eva **67**
Iggie's House **53**
Illustrated Dictionary
of Science **102**
Imaginary Menagerie **94**
Impey, Rose **39,46**
In Time of War **93**
Incredible Cross-Sections **102**
Incredible Journey **56**
Indian in the Cupboard **52**
Inkpen, Mick **7,14,19,21**
Ireson, Barbara **39**
Irish Folktales **45**
Iron Man **67**
Iron Woman **67**
Island of Adventure **53**
It Was a Dark and Stormy Night **35**
It Was Jake **20**
Jackson, Steve **67**
Jacques, Brian **68,69**
Jaffrey, Madhur **48**
Jamaica's Find **18**

James & the Giant Peach **59**
James, Simon **20**
Janine & the New Baby **25**
Jansson, Tove **68**
Jarvis, Robin **68**
Jasper's Beanstalk **14**
Jeffers, Susan **31**
Jennings, Paul **68**
Jeram, Anita **20**
Jeremiah in the Dark Woods **35**
Jets **33**
Jim & the Beanstalk **31**
Jolly Postman **9**
Jolly Roger **32**
Jones, Diana Wynne **70**
Jones, Terry **46,70**
Josie Smith **41**
Julian Stories **36**
Jungle Book **71**
Jungman, Ann **39**
Just So Stories **71**
Juster, Norman **70**
Kaleidoscopes **99**
Karate Princess, The **42**
Kastner, Eric **70**
Katie Morag and the Two
Grandmothers **18**
Kay, Jackie **94**
Kelly, Fiona **70**
Kemp, Gene **70**
Kerr, Judith **20,70**
King Arthur **48**
King-Smith, Dick **39,71**
King, Clive **70**
Kipling, Rudyard **71**
Kipper's Toybox **19**
Kitamura, Satoshi **22**
Kittens in the Kitchen **60**
Krindlekrax **78**
Ladybird **7,33**
Ladybird Moves Home **10**
Laird, Elizabeth **71**
Langley, Jonathan **9**
Last Vampire **65**
Lavelle, Sheila **40**
Lawrence, Louise **109**
Layton, George **72**
Lear, Edward **94**
Lee, Alan **48**
Leitch, Patricia **72**
Let the Circle be Unbroken **112**
Letterland ABC **8**
Lewis, CS **72**
Lighthouse Keeper's Lunch **12**
Lindgren, Astrid **72**
Lingard, Joan **109**
Lion at School **41**
The Lion, the Witch
& the Wardrobe **72**
Listen to the Dark **66**
Lister, Robin **48**

Little House in the Big Woods **85**
Little Love Song **109**
Little Princess **56**
Little Vampire, The **81**
Little White Horse **65**
Little Women **51**
Lively, Penelope **72**
Lives of Christopher Chant **70**
Livingstone, Ian **67**
Lofting, Hugh **72**
Low Tide **75**
Lowry, Lois **72,109**
Lucky **94**
Lucy & Tom's ABC **8**
Macaulay, David **102**
Machine Gunners **85**
MacMonagle, Niall **93**
MacPherson, Ann **113**
Madame Doubtfire **108**
Magic Finger **37**
Magorian, Michelle **72,73,109**
Mahy, Margaret **22,73,109**
Maisy **10**
Make Like a Tree and Leave **60**
Making Out **114**
Malcolm, Jahnna **73**
Man Whose Mother
Was A Pirate **22**
Man, The **56**
Maphead **109**
Marianne Dreams **82**
Mark, Jan **73,109**
Marshall, James Vance **73**
Martin, Ann M **73**
Mary Poppins **83**
Masefield, John **75**
Matilda **59**
Matterson, Elizabeth **9**
Mayle, Peter **100**
Mayne, William **75**
Mayo, Margaret **46,48**
McCaughrean, Geraldine **48,86**
McCaughrean, Tom **75**
McFarlane, Aidan **113**
McGough, Roger **75,91,94**
McKay, Hilary **75**
McKee, David **7,22,23**
McNaughton, Colin **32,33,94**
Meg & Mog **22**
Melusine **105**
Memoirs of a
Dangerous Alien **78**
Mennyms, The **85**
Meredith, Susan **100**
Meteorite Spoon **78**
Micklethwait, Lucy **99**
Midnight Blue **62**
Miffy **14**
Miller, Virginia **8**
Milligan, Spike **95**

Milly Molly Mandy **36**
Milne, AA **7,75,95**
Mog the Forgetful Cat **20**
Monkey Island **62**
Montgomery, LM **75**
Moondial **58**
Mooney, Bel **40**
Moonfleet **61**
Moon, Pat **75**
Moore, Inga **22**
Morpurgo, Michael **40,76**
Most Amazing Hide and
Seek ABC **10**
Most Amazing Pop-Up
Science Book **102**
Mother Goose **9**
Mouse & His Child **66**
Mousehole Cat **12**
Mr Little's Noisy Boat **16**
Mr Magnolia **13**
Mr Majeika **36**
Mrs Frisby & the
Rats of NIMH **77**
Mrs Pepperpot **41**
Ms Wiz **35**
Mummy Laid An Egg **31**
Munsch, Robert **22**
Murphy, Jill **22,40**
My Best Fiend **40**
My First Book of Time **7**
My First Word Book **7**
My Mate Shofiq **76**
My Naughty Little Sister **37**
My Teacher is an Alien **58**
Myths & Legends **47**
Nabb, Magdalen **41**
Napper Goes for Goals **85**
Nation, Terry **76**
Naughty Stories **39**
Naughton, Bill **76**
Necklace of Raindrops **51**
Needle, Jan **76**
Nesbit, E **76**
Nichols, Grace **92**
Nicoll, Helen **22**
Niffs & Whiffs **92**
Nimmo, Jenny **41**
Noah's Ark **16**
Norton, Mary **77**
Not Dressed Like That
you Don't! **106**
Not Now Bernard **22**
Now We are Six **95**
Nursery Board Books **7**
Nursery Rhymes **9**
O'Brien, Robert **77**
O'Hara, Elizabeth **110**
Oi, Get Off Our Train **14**
Old Bear **18**
Oliver's Vegetables **18**
On the Way Home **22**

On Your Potty **8**
One More River **105**
One Snowy Night **14**
Outsiders, The **108**
Owl Who was Afraid of
the Dark **42**
Owl & the Pussycat **94**
Oxenbury, Helen **24,25,26**
Paddington **35**
Paper Faces **51**
Paperbag Princess **22**
Parcel of Patterns **85**
Pascal, Francine **77**
Patchwork Cat **12**
Patchwork Quilt **31**
Paterson, Katherine **77**
Patten, Brian **89,96**
Paulsen, Gary **110,111**
Paul, Korky **24**
Pearce, Philippa **41,77**
Peepo **12**
Pelham, David **10**
Penguin Small **20**
Peppermint Pig **52**
Peter Pan **52**
Peter & the Wolf **13**
Phantom Tollbooth **70**
Pienkowski, Jan **7,10,22**
Pigeon Summer **83**
Pigman, The **113**
Pilling, Ann **77**
Pippi Longstocking **72**
Playtime Treasury **9**
Please Mrs Butler **93**
Poetry Jump Up **92**
Poetry Paintbox series **92**
Pongwiffy **83**
Potter, Beatrix **24**
Prelutsky, Jack **9,89**
Price, Willard **78**
Princess Smartypants **16**
Prince, Maggie **78**
Proper Little Nooryeff **112**
Proysen, Alf **41**
Puzzle Adventures **78**
Quantock Quartet **108**
Queen's Nose **71**
Railway Cat **35**
Railway Children **76**
Rainforest **16**
Ramona Quimby Aged 8 **57**
Ransome, Arthur **78**
Rats **38**
Read Aloud Rhymes for
the Very Young **9**
Real Cool **93**
Rebecca's World **76**
Red Nose Readers **33**
Redwall series **68**
Revolting Bridesmaids **38**
Revolting Rhymes **94**

Rhymes & Lullabies **9**
Rhyme Stew **94**
Ridley, Philip **74,78**
Rix, Jamie **78**
Road to Memphis **112**
Robin Hood **47**
Roll of Thunder Hear
My Cry **112**
Room 13 – **83**
Rosen, Michael **24,86,91,96**
Rosie's Walk **19**
Ross, Tony **8,24,27**
Round, Graham **78**
Rudley Cabot **56**
Rumblefish **109**
Run with the Wind **75**
Runaways, The **83**
Sackful of Stories **86**
Saga of Erik the Viking **70**
Sage, Alison **86**
Salisbury, Graham **110**
Sam the Girl Detective **36**
Sam's Sandwich **10**
Scare Yourself to Sleep **39**
Scarecrows **112**
School **31**
School at the Chalet **55**
Scieszka, Jon **25,32**
Scottish Folktales **47,45**
Scott, Hugh **110**
Seasons of Spendour **48**
Secret Clues **70**
Secret Garden **56**
Secret of Platform 13 **67**
Secret, The **83**
See Ya Simon **66**
Sefton, Catherine **42**
Sendak, Maurice **25**
Serrallier, Ian **79**
Seuss, Dr **33**
Sewell, Anna **79**
Shakespeare, William **79**
Sheep Pig **71**
Sheldon, Diane **25**
Sherlock, Philip **47**
Shrinking of Treehorn **38**
Silly Verse for Kids **95**
Silver Sword **79**
Simmonds, Posy **32**
Simon and the Witch **35**
Simon, Francesca **42**
Simpkin **13**
Six Dinner Sid **22**
Sleigh, Barbara **79**
Smith, Dodie **81**
Smith, Lane **25,32**
Snape, Charles & Juliet **81**
Snapshot Board Books **7**
Snowman, The **13**
Snow, Alan **32,45**
Soccer at Sandford **57**

Somer-Bodenberg, Angela **81**
Sophie series **39**
Spooky stories **86**
Sprinters **33**
Spyri, Johanna **81**
Stannard, Russell **80,81**
Starring Sally J Freedman
as Herself **53**
Steps up the Chimney **57**
Stevenson, RL **82**
Stig of the Dump **70**
Stine, RL **82**
Stinky Cheeseman **32**
Stone Cold **110**
Stone Mouse **41**
Stories from the Ballet **86**
Storr, Catherine **42,82**
Story of Tracy Beaker **86**
Strachan, Ian **110**
Streatfeild, Noel **82**
Street Child **61**
Strong, Jeremy **42**
Suitcase Kid **86**
Sun Horse, Moon Horse **82**
Sutcliff, Rosemary **48,82**
Swallows & Amazons **78**
Swan Sister **59**
Swindells, Robert **82, 110,112**
Sword in the Stone **85**
Tales of a Fourth Grade
Nothing **53**
Talking Turkeys **96**
Tarka the Otter **85**
Tasting the Thunder **110**
Taylor, Mildred D **112**
Taylor, Theodore **83**
Thawing Frozen Frogs **96**
There's an Awful Lot of Weirdos in
our Neighbourhood **94**
They Do Things Differently
There **110**
Thirteen Something **113**
This Little Puffin **9**
This Poem Doesn't Rhyme **92**
Thomas the Tank Engine **12**
Thomas, Iolette **25**
Thomas, Ruth **63,83**
Thomas, Valerie **24**
Thomson, Pat **86**
Thomson, Ruth **113**
Threadbear **20**
Three Little Wolves & the
Big Bad Pig **25**
Thunder & Lightnings **73**
Tiger Eyes **105**
Tiger Who came to Tea **20**
Tintin **66**
Tomlinson, Jill **42**
Tom's Midnight Garden **77**
Townsend, Sue **112**
Traveller in Time **83**

Travers, PL **83**
Treasure Island **82**
Tripods Trilogy **57**
Trivizas, Eugene **25**
Trouble with Donovan Croft **52**
Trouble with Mum **15**
True Story of the Three
Little Pigs **25**
Tunnel, The **26**
Turbulent Term of Tyke Tiler **70**
Turnbull, Ann **83**
Twelfth Day of July **109**
Two Weeks with the Queen **64**
Two's Company **94**
Umansky, Kaye **83**
Uncle Albert series **81**
Understanding The Facts of Life **100**
Under the Blood Red Sun **110**
Under the Hawthorn Tree **57**
Uderzo **64**
Ungerer, Tomi **36**
Unreal **68**
Ure, Jean **112**
Uttley, Alison **83**
Varley, Susan **26**
Velveteen Rabbit **26**
Very First Poetry Book **89**
Verne, Jules **83**
Very Hungry Caterpillar **15**
Vipont, Elfrida **26**
Vlad the Drac.**39**
Voce Louise **94**
Voigt, Cynthia **112**
Waddell, Martin **26,28,85**
Walkabout **73**
Walker Book of Fairytales **46**
Walker Book of Poetry for
Children **89**
Walsh, Jill Paton **85**
War Boy **62**
Warlock of Firetop Mountain **67**
Watanabe, Sheigo **9**
Watership Down **51**
Waugh, Sylvia **84,85**
Ways Things Work **102**
Way to Sattin Shore **77**
Webb, Kaye **91**
We Hate Ballet **73**
Weirdstone of Brisingamen **62**
Welcome to the Dead House **82**
Welsh Folk Tales **45**
We're Going on a Bear Hunt **24**
Westall, Robert **85, 112**
West Indian Folk Tales **47**
Whale's Song **25**
What Katy Did **57**
What's Happening To Me **100**
Wheels on Bus **12**
When Hitler Stole Pink Rabbit **70**
When Sheep Cannot Sleep **22**
When We Were Very Young **95**

When You Can't Say No **108**
Where Did I Come From **100**
Where's Spot **18**
Where The Wild Things Are **25**
Where's Julius **14**
Where's My Teddy **12**
Where's Wally **65**
Which Witch **67**
Whispers in the Graveyard **55**
White, EB **85**
White, TH **85**
Why the Whales Came **76**
Why Weeps the Brogan **110**
Wibbly Pig **7**
Wilde, Nicholas **85**
Wilde, Oscar **46**
Wilkes, Angela **7**
Wilder, Laura Ingalls **85**
Wildsmith, Brian **26**
Williamson, Henry **85**
Williams, Marcia **33,47**
Williams, Marjorie **26**
Williams, Sarah **9**
Williams, Ursula Moray **42**
Willis, Jeanne **27**
Willy the Wimp **13**
Wilson, Barbara Ker **47**
Wilson, David Henry **54,86**
Wilson, Jacqueline **86,113**
Wind in the Willows **65**
Winnie the Pooh **7,75**
Winnie the Witch **24**
Witches (Dahl) **59**
Witches (Hawkins) **66**
Wizard of Earthsea **65**
Wizard of Oz **52**
Wolves of Willoughby Chase **51**
Wondercrump Poetry **91**
Woof! **51**
Wool Pack **65**
World Religions **102**
Worst Witch **40**
Wreck of the Zanzibar **76**
Wright, Christopher **100**
Wright, Kit **96**
Young, Jay **102**
Young Selina **46**
Z for Zachariah **77**
Zacharias, Thomas **27**
Zelinsky, Paul **12**
Zephaniah, Benjamin **96**
Zindel, Paul **113**
Zlata's Diary **108**
Zwerger, Lisbeth **45**

WHERE TO FIND YOUR NEAREST WATERSTONE'S

ABERDEEN
236 Union Street
Aberdeen AB1 1TN
Tel: 01224 571655

BATH
4 Milsom Street
Bath BA1 1DA
Tel: 01225 448515

University of Bath
Claverton Down
Bath BA2 7JZ
Tel: 01225 465565

BELFAST
Queen's Building
8 Royal Avenue
Belfast BT1 1DA
Tel: 01232 247355

BEXLEYHEATH
75 The Mall
Broadway Shopping Centre
Bexleyheath
Kent DA6 7JJ
Tel: 0181 3014411

BIRMINGHAM
24 High Street
Birmingham B4 7SL
Tel: 0121 6334353
Young Waterstone's
Tel: 0121 6161557

BOURNEMOUTH
14/16 The Arcade
Bournemouth
BH1 2AH
Tel: 01202 299449

BRADFORD
University of Bradford
Great Horton Road
Bradford BD7 1DS
Tel: 01274 727885

Management Centre
Bookshop
Emm Lane
Bradford BD7 4JL
Tel: 01274 481404

BRIGHTON
55 North Street
Brighton
East Sussex BN1 1RH
Tel: 01273 327867

BRISTOL
27 College Green
Bristol
Avon BS1 5TD
Tel: 0117 9250511

Computer Centre
University of Bristol
Tyndall Avenue
Bristol BS8 1TW
Tel: 0117 9254297

The Galleries
Broadmead
Bristol
Avon BS1 3XD
Tel: 0117 9252274

BROMLEY
20 Market Square
Bromley
Kent BR1 1NA
Tel: 0181 464 6562

CAMBRIDGE
6 Bridge Street
Cambridge CB2 1UA
Tel: 01223 300123

CANTERBURY
20 St. Margaret's Street
Canterbury
Kent CT1 2XH
Tel: 01227 456343

CARDIFF
2a The Hayes
Cardiff CF1 2AH
Tel: 01222 665606

CHELTENHAM
88 The Promenade
Cheltenham
GL50 1NB
Tel: 01242 512722

CHESTER
43 Bridge Street Row
Chester CH1 1NW
Tel: 01244 328040

COLCHESTER
The Old Library
16 Culver Precinct
Colchester
Essex CO1 1JQ
Tel: 01206 767623

University of Essex
Wivenhoe Park
Colchester
Essex CO4 3SQ
Tel: 01206 864773

CORK
69 Patrick Street
Cork
Eire
Tel: 010 353 21 267522

Boole Library
Basement
University College Cork
Cork
Eire
Tel: 101 353 21 276575

CROYDON
1063 Whitgift Centre
Croydon
Surrey CR0 1UX
Tel: 0181 686 7032

DERBY
78 - 80 St. Peter's Street
Derby
Tel: 01332 296997

DORKING
54 South Street
Dorking
Surrey RH4 2HQ
Tel: 01306 886884

DUBLIN
7 Dawson Street
Dublin 2
Tel: 010 353 16 791260

DUNDEE
35 Commercial Street
Dundee DD1 3DG
Tel: 01382 200322

DURHAM
69 Saddler Street
Durham DH1 3NP
Tel: 0191 3831488

EASTBOURNE
120 Terminus Road
Eastbourne BN21 3AJ
Tel: 01323 735676

EDINBURGH
128 Princes Street
Edinburgh EH2 4AD
Tel: 0131 2262666

13 Princes Street
Edinburgh EH2 2AN
Tel: 0131 5563034/5

83 George Street
Edinburgh EH2 3ES
Tel: 0131 2253436

EPSOM
113 High Street
Epsom
KT19 8DT
Tel: 01372 741713

EXETER
48 High Street
Exeter
Devon EX4 3DJ
Tel: 01392 218392

GATESHEAD
17 The Parade
Metro Centre
Gateshead NE11 9YJ
Tel: 0191 4932715

GATWICK
North Terminal Airside
Gatwick Airport
Gatwick
West Sussex RH6 0NP
Tel: 01293 507112

GLASGOW
132 Union Street
Glasgow G1 3QH
Tel: 0141 2210890

45 Princes Square
Glasgow G1 3JN
Tel: 0141 2219650

GUILDFORD
20 The Friary
Guildford
Surrey GU1 4YN
Tel: 01483 502801

35 North Street
Guildford
Surrey GU1 4TE
Tel: 01483 302919

HANLEY
The Tontines Centre
Parliament Row
Hanley
Stoke-on-Trent
ST1 1PW
Tel: 01782 204582

HULL
University of Hull
University House

Hull HU6 7RX
Tel: 01482 444190

The Grand Buildings
Jameson Street
Hull
Tel: 01482 580234

IPSWICH
15 -19 Buttermarket
Ipswich
Suffolk
IP1 1BQ
Tel: 01473 289044

KINGSTON
23 Thames Street
Kingston-upon-Thames
Surrey
Tel: 0181 5471221

LANCASTER
2 King Street
Lancaster LA1 1JN
Tel: 01524 61477

LEEDS
36 Albion Street
Leeds LS1 6HX
Tel: 0113 2420839

93 Albion Street
Leeds LS1 5AP
Tel: 0113 2444588

LEICESTER
The Shires
Churchgate
Leicester
Tel: 0116 2516838

LIVERPOOL
52 Bold Street
Liverpool L1 4EA
Tel: 0151 7090866

LONDON

CAMDEN
128 High Street
London NW1 0NB
Tel: 0171 2844948

CHARING CROSS ROAD
121 Charing Cross Road
London WC2H 0EA
Tel: 0171 4344291

COVENT GARDEN
9 Garrick Street
London WC2 4LA
Tel: 0171 8366757

EARL'S COURT
266 Earl's Court Road
London SW5 9AS
Tel: 0171 3701616

GOLDSMITH'S
Goldsmith's College
New Cross
London SE14 6NW
Tel: 0181 4690262

HAMPSTEAD
68 Hampstead High Street
London NW3 1QP
Tel: 0171 7941098